169

World Bank Discussion Papers

Common Property Resources

A Missing Dimension of Development Strategies

N. S. Jodha

The World Bank
Washington, D.C.

First printing August 1992

Discussion Papers present results of country analysis or research that is circulated to encourage discussion and comment within the development community. To present these results with the least possible delay, the typescript of this paper has not been prepared in accordance with the procedures appropriate to formal printed texts, and the World Bank accepts no responsibility for errors.

The findings, interpretations, and conclusions expressed in this paper are entirely those of the author(s) and should not be attributed in any manner to the World Bank, to its affiliated organizations, or to members of its Board of Executive Directors or the countries they represent. The World Bank does not guarantee the accuracy of the data included in this publication and accepts no responsibility whatsoever for any consequence of their use. Any maps that accompany the text have been prepared solely for the convenience of readers; the designations and presentation of material in them do not imply the expression of any opinion whatsoever on the part of the World Bank, its affiliates, or its Board or member countries concerning the legal status of any country, territory, city, or area or of the authorities thereof or concerning the delimitation of its boundaries or its national affiliation.

The complete backlist of publications from the World Bank is shown in the annual *Index of Publications,* which contains an alphabetical title list (with full ordering information) and indexes of subjects, authors, and countries and regions. The latest edition is available free of charge from the Distribution Unit, Office of the Publisher, Department F, The World Bank, 1818 H Street, N.W., Washington, D.C. 20433, U.S.A., or from Publications, The World Bank, 66, avenue d'Iéna, 75116 Paris, France.

ISSN: 0259-210X

N. S. Jodha is head of the Farming Systems Division of the International Center for Integrated Mountain Development.

Library of Congress Cataloging-in-Publication Data

Jodha, N. S.
Common property resources : a missing dimension of development strategies / N.S. Jodha.
p. cm. — (World Bank discussion papers ; 169)
Includes bibliographical references.
ISBN 0-8213-2146-3
1. Natural resources—Developing countries—Management. 2. Public goods. 3. Community development—Developing countries. 4. Rural poor—Developing countries. I. Title. II. Series.
HC59.7.J57 1992
338.9'009172'4—dc20 92-16722
CIP

ABSTRACT

Common Property Resources (CPRs) continue to be an important part of communities' natural resource endowment in developing countries. Despite their valuable contributions to people's sustenance, environmental stability and the strengthening of private resource based farming systems, they are neglected by researchers, policy makers and development planners alike. Disregard of CPRs and their productive potential is a major missing dimension of rural development strategies in developing countries and reflects much of the officialdom's indifference to environmental protection. This is illustrated by the status and changes in CPRs in the dry tropical regions of India, where not only are CPRs not integrated into rural development strategies but they are left prone to rapid degradation largely induced by side effects of other development and welfare policies.

The paper argues that due to the convergence between potential CPR-centered policies/programs and the emerging concerns for participatory development, environmental sustainability and poverty alleviation, CPRs could be made an effective component of rural development strategies in areas such as the dry regions of India.

The paper reports and analyzes the empirical findings from a study of CPRs conducted by the author while working at ICRISAT during the 1980s. Based on four years of field work covering 82 villages in over 20 districts of India's dry region, the study has quantified the benefits of CPRs in terms of employment, income and physical supplies, and has recorded some less quantifiable contributions.

The study reveals that relatively poor households depend more on CPRs. They receive the bulk of their fuel supplies and fodder from CPRs. CPR product collection is an important source of employment and income, especially during the periods when other opportunities are almost non-existent. Furthermore, although likely to be under-estimated, CPR income accounts for 14 to 23 percent of household income from all other sources in the study villages. More importantly, the inclusion of CPR income in total household incomes from other sources, reduces the extent of rural income inequalities, as indicated by lower values of the Gini-coefficient. In the case of poor households, per worker employment days generated by CPRs are higher than the employment available on families' own farm or even on the public works programs. CPRs contributions to private resource based farming systems are also very significant. About 31 to 42 percent of non-purchased farm inputs during different stages of cropping season are provided by CPRs in cash or kind. The less quantifiable gains of CPRs relate to the health and stability of environmental resources at the village level. The paper gives a descriptive account of some of them.

Despite these gains, CPRs are facing serious decline. The study records the massive decline in the area of CPRs, physical degradation and disruption of traditional management systems for CPRs due to public policies and side effects of rural transformation. During 1951-52 to 1982-84, the area of CPRs in the study villages had declined by 31 to 52 percent.

Similarly, most of the villages have given up traditional CPR management practices involving protection, development and usage regulation, thus converting CPR into open access regime.

The final impact of these changes include the over-exploitation and degradation of CPRs as indicated by reduced biomass productivity and other contributions characteristic of healthy CPRs.

These unfavorable changes are a product of the combined impact of state policies, market integration, and demographic, economic and institutional changes at the village level. State land policies have encouraged privatization of CPRs through legal and extra-legal means. They disrupted the traditional management systems for CPRs without providing any effective substitute. Public measures to raise the productivity of these resources over-emphasized technological components, disregarding their CPR-dimensions. This is why many have proven to be ineffective.

The decline and degradation of CPRs in a way reflect an unquantified process of pauperization of rural communities and degradation of environment at the micro level. Accordingly, the reduced productivity of CPRs and increasingly inferior options offered by them on the one hand, and an increasing number of people that depend on them on the other are true indicators of pauperization in rural communities. The adverse effects of CPR decline on private resource based farming and on the environment have severe long term implications, but they are not reflected in any social accounting matrix.

At the village level, ecological, demographic and market related factors influence people's approach to CPRs in different ways. The study identified and recorded such differences. The smaller villages, more distant from markets, continue to protect CPRs well. Similarly, within the same villages, some people care more about productive CPR units than others. In some cases enlightened villagers and NGOs have helped to rehabilitate CPRs. Encouragement of these processes can help develop CPRs for sustainable use. In general people have adjusted to their decline either through increased resignation or through over-extraction of the remaining CPRs. However, there are some cases where communities have shown positive concern for CPRs and resisted impact of factors adversely affecting CPRs.

This may offer certain leads for evolving effective CPR-strategies for the future, a matter on which there is an ongoing debate and controversy in the development literature.

In this controversy, certain arguments emphasize the unavoidable impacts of market oriented development, population induced land scarcity, and the economic inefficiency of resource use under common property regimes. Such arguments do not portray a bright future for CPRs. This paper questions the basis of these arguments, by highlighting the positive features and contributions of CPRs, which should form the basis of interventions for their protection, development and sustainable use. There are important factors that plead for the integration of CPRs into resource-centered development strategies.

Besides the contributions made by CPRs to the economy of rural people, increasing concerns for participatory development and environmentally friendly natural resource management systems strengthen the case for a new look at the development potential of CPRs. The focal areas for a positive approach to CPRs are: (i) public policies to protect CPR area and facilitate emergence of local initiatives to regulate their usage; (ii) new technological elements; (iii) investment support to raise productivity of CPRs to break the vicious circle of "low productivity -- over extraction -- degradation -- further lower productivity"; (iv) management of CPRs through the promotion of CPR-user groups, since the key need facing CPRs is to regulate their use, which is even more pressing than technology and investment. Based on local socioeconomic and environmental circumstances and learning from the successful cases of natural resource management involving local communities and NGOs, CPR user groups can be promoted. The paper also lists possible obstacles to such initiatives.

Donor agencies that have shown indifference to CPRs in the past can play an important role in the rehabilitation and development of CPRs as productive community resources. The case for CPRs fits quite well with the recent concerns of donor groups and other development agencies in the field of poverty alleviation, participatory development and environmental protection emphasized by their policies. However, policy makers need to have a correct understanding of current CPR-issues, constraints and needs, perspective when dealing with village level natural resource development, to ensure that they capture rather than overlook and lose the development potential of common property resources.

ACKNOWLEDGMENT

This paper is based on the author's study on Common Property Resources conducted over several years during the 1980s, particularly while working at the International Crops Research Institute for Semi-arid Tropics (ICRISAT). The work was also facilitated through a small but highly flexible grant from the Ford Foundation. I would like to record my appreciation for both organizations, and particularly for Jim Ryan and Tom Walker at ICRISAT and Robert Chambers and Deep Joshi at the Ford Foundation.

Most grateful thanks are due to my more than thirty assistants and cooperators in the field investigations that I carried out in 82 villages scattered over half a dozen linguistic areas and agroclimatic zones in India. Many of them shared neither my language nor my background, and yet joined in our common concern for CPRs; many of them might neither read, nor understand this acknowledgment and yet, in my mind, deserve it most. I would also like to acknowledge the contribution of various organizations in India and abroad, including NGOs, to which I presented the evidence collected in the field and which instigated me to rework my analysis and argument, in order to make the understanding of CPR issues simpler and operational.

My special thanks go to Michael M. Cernea and Scott Guggenheim at the World Bank, who gave me valuable comments and induced me to prepare for publication this overall synthesis of my past research and analyses on CPRs. Thanks for useful suggestions are due also to H. Binswanger, H. Daly, R. Grimshaw, J. Warford, and to several participants in a sociological seminar at the World Bank, where an earlier version of this paper was presented.

Finally, I would like to express my gratitude to Sami Joshi and Gracie M. Ochieng who tirelessly processed different drafts of this paper and its not-so-simple tables.

FOREWORD

The research on common property systems in the dry areas of rural India, carried out by Dr. N.S. Jodha and his team, is the most comprehensive and systematic analysis of natural resources under common property regimes available in the recent scientific literature. The study addresses the crucial links between poverty, social organizations of resource use, and environmental management. Based on the body of quantitative and qualitative data that his research has generated, Dr. Jodha documents both the major contributions provided by common property resources and the unprecedented stresses which they currently face.

The present synthesis study, as well as studies by other social and environmental scientists, have demonstrated a close link between common property resources (CPRs) and the survival systems of significant numbers of the rural poor. Around the world, socioeconomic research has documented that not just the landless but also the landed poor, especially women, depend largely on community lands and resources for food, fiber, fuel, and income. Replacing common property through individual titling or transfer of ownership to the state, far from improving resource management, has usually led to an aggravation of poverty and a concomitant deterioration of the environment.

However, confronted by the internal pressures of population growth and external intrusion, previously stable forms of common resource management are increasingly breaking down and in fact becoming open access resources, with consequent environmental degradation. Because of this physical depletion of the commons and the breakdown of equitable patterns of distribution, the poorest strata are deprived of a substantial portion of their economic base. Extensive exploitation and mining of the diminishing resources result in accelerated environmental degradation and heightened poverty.

Dr. Jodha's study thus highlights policy issues significant for both planners and development theorists. Policy research is needed to point ways in which common property systems can be strengthened and improved. As Dr. Jodha correctly notes, donor agencies have a particular responsibility, not just to avoid harming CPR systems but to develop and promote the social and environmental technologies needed to sustain them in the face of new challenges.

Several new projects assisted by the World Bank in India, the Philippines, the Amazon and elsewhere explicitly seek to assist CPR systems adapt to changing conditions. Although still young, preliminary results already point to a heightened role for the international community in supporting improved patterns of local resource management. Studies, such as Dr. Jodha's, thus become both diagnostic and prescriptive in their lessons and are important steps forward in our understanding of the intimate connections between environment, social organization, and poverty alleviation.

We are therefore pleased to publish the present study in the World Bank Discussion Paper series, for further public debate and analysis of the important issues it raises. Additional studies in this series will follow, in our effort to advance the frontier of knowledge, the policies, and best practices for sustainable development.

Mohamed T. El-Ashry
Director
Environment Department
The World Bank

TABLE OF CONTENTS

Page

LIST OF TABLES/FIGURES

COMMON PROPERTY RESOURCES: A MISSING DIMENSION OF DEVELOPMENT STRATEGIES

1. INTRODUCTION

The rather mixed success of even well supported rural development interventions has been a long standing concern of development and donor agencies. The failures are more conspicuous where the central role in the development processes is played by institutional as opposed to technological factors; group action as against individual initiatives; participatory processes versus externally initiated and controlled activities; the sustainable use and management of a resource base as against short term productivity promotion; fragile and high risk environments as against stable prime areas.

Responses to such failures often repeat the history in one way or the other by: emphasizing technological remedies to handle what are primarily institutional problems; strengthening physical infrastructure and imposing formal legal restrictions as substitutes for people's organizations; bribing people through a variety of subsidies to induce their participation; and (in some cases) dropping the problem altogether by declaring it a hopeless situation beyond redemption.

Without belittling the importance of technology, support systems and incentives, it may be stated that the misplaced emphasis on the above responses distorts the perspectives on the problems at hand and their possible solutions. Most importantly, it tends to block the opportunity to properly assess the ecological and institutional context of the situation and to understand people's traditional resource management and production strategies. These can offer useful leads for evolving workable options, (especially in the situations considered "hopeless") through conventional development approaches. An illustration of many of these features is the way in which common property resources (CPRs) are treated or disregarded in rural development programs in most of developing countries.

Common property resources (CPRs) can be broadly defined as those resources in which a group of people have co-equal use rights, specifically rights that exclude the use of those resources by other people. Individuals' membership in the group of co-owners is typically conferred by membership in some other group, generally a group whose central purpose is not the use or administration of the resource (*per se*), such as a village, tribe, etc. (Magrath 1986, Ostrom 1986 and 1988, Bromley and Cernea 1989).

Common property resources are an important component of the natural resource endowment of rural communities in developing countries. Unlike in high income countries, in the case of developing countries CPRs continue to be a significant component of the land resources base of rural communities. This is more so in the relatively high risk, low productivity areas such as the arid and semi-arid tropical regions of India and several African countries (Sandford 1983). Historically, the circumstances favorable to common property resources in these areas (Table 1) included: (i) the presence of factors less favorable to rapid privatization of land resources; (ii) community level concerns for collective sustenance and ecological fragility; and (iii) dependence of private farming on the collective risk sharing arrangements.

Table 1

CIRCUMSTANCES HISTORICALLY ASSOCIATED WITH THE COMMON PROPERTY RESOURCES IN DRY REGIONS OF INDIA

NATURAL RESOURCE BASE AND AGRO-ECOLOGICAL FEATURES

Low and variable precipitation; heterogenous (including submarginal fragile land) resources; nature's low regeneration capacities; limited and high risk production options; etc.

IMPLICATIONS/IMPERATIVES

• Low population pressure; market isolation; limited technological and institutional interventions	• Heterogeneity, fragility of resource base; inadequacy of private risk strategies;	• Narrow, unstable production base; diversified, biomass centered, land extensive farming systems.
• Limited incentives and compulsions for privatization of CPRs	• Balancing extensive-intensive land uses; focus on collective risk sharing.	• Reliance on collective measures against seasonality and risk.
• Circumstances favorable to CPRs.	• Community sanctions for CPRs (protection, access usage, etc.).	• Complementarity of CPR-PPR based activities.[a]

a/ PPR = Private Property Resources.

However, for a variety of causes, both historical and ongoing, which will be discussed in this paper, common property regimes over natural resources have been undergoing continuous erosion, degradation and transformation into open access regimes. Concomitantly, and despite their significant contribution to the sustenance of rural households and their potential role in equitable and participatory development, CPRs have been largely ignored by policy makers, researchers, planners and donors alike. Even when development interventions are focussed on a physical/natural resource of the community (e.g., village pasture, forest, etc.) predicated on a common property management regime, their CPR dimension is seldom considered systematically. Consequently, despite technological inputs or sometimes financial support, CPRs continue to be degraded and disappear. "The tragedy of the commons" is used as a convenient cover-up formula for the default and insensitivity of public interventions to these resources (Feeny et al. 1990).

The present paper describes the CPR situation in the dry tropical regions of India, where public policies and programs have not only failed to recognize and harness the potential of CPRs, but have in effect operated against them. These regions which extend over 150 districts, account for above 43 percent of India's total geographical area and 31 percent of its total rural population (Jodha 1989c). In Indian villages, CPRs include community pastures, community forests, wastelands, common dumping and threshing grounds, watershed drainages and village ponds, rivers, rivulets as well as their banks and beds. Even when the formal legal ownership of some of these resources rests with certain agencies (e.g., waste lands that belong to the state revenue department), in a *de facto* sense they belong to village communities. The field level evidence presented here on different aspects of CPRs has been corroborated by other micro-level studies on the subject in different parts of the dry regions of India. (Iyengar 1988; Brara 1987; Chen 1988; Blaikie et al. 1985; Gupta 1986; Wade 1988; Ananth Ram and Kalla 1988; and Oza 1989).

In the following section, we introduce the study areas, data base, and methodological highlights of the field work that undergird the analysis. Section three presents quantified details of the contributions of CPRs to village economies. Section four discusses the changing status of CPRs in terms of the decline in their area, productivity and management systems. Section five identifies the various causal factors in the decline of CPRs. Section six discusses the people's responses to the changing situation of CPRs. Section seven comments on the future prospects of CPRs in dry regions of India. Section eight discusses the policy implications, for governments and donor agencies, of the major issues highlighted by the paper, with a special emphasis on action to rehabilitate CPRs.

2. DATA BASE AND METHODOLOGY

2.1 AREA AND INFORMATION COVERAGE

The evidence presented in this paper is based on the field studies of CPRs conducted during the author's work at ICRISAT. The village and farm level data were collected over a period of four years -- 1982-1986 -- and the analysis of those findings has continued up to this present paper. Additional data have become available through the work of other researchers and are referred to and discussed in the paper. The field data generated by the author's studies refer to 82 villages from 21 districts, scattered in seven major states in the dry tropical zone of India. Map 1 indicates the location of districts and number of study villages. Annex 1 provides some overall agro-ecological, demographic, administrative, and CPR related details of the areas studied.

Data collection was carried out through different methods that included structured surveys, physical verification/measurement and regular monitoring, recording of oral histories and participant observations by (heterogeneous in terms of background and age) teams of formal and informal research assistants and cooperators in each district. Information was supplemented by detailed longitudinal data available from ICRISAT's village level studies, (Singh et al. 1985) conducted in ten villages of five districts,which were also covered by the CPR studies. The number of units (e.g., villages, households, CPR-units, etc.) covered by different investigations will be indicated while reporting the results.

The study areas were selected purposively, with two important preconditions: (i) representativeness for zones with different soils, agro-climatic features and population densities; and (ii) availability of local assistants to help in the fieldwork. The latter was a logistic requirement imposed by the nature of the studies. The CPR studies, unlike routine agro-economic surveys, required greater flexibility and use of unconventional methods of information gathering on the one hand, and close familiarity of investigators with the villages and their oral history on the other. Because of the latter, identification of relevant assistants from different agro-climatic zones preceded the purposive selection of study areas (Jodha 1986).

Apart from these features, the approach and methodology of CPR research were unconventional in several other ways. The important ones are stated below.

2.2 THEORETICAL FRAMEWORK

While existing theories and concepts in the literature on property rights and regimes were taken into account, the dictates of dominant theories were not allowed to constrain the approach of studies. Accordingly, rather than trying to confirm or reject specific hypotheses, the focus of the research was on the past and present status, management and productivity of community resources in the villages. The legal provisions that bestowed ownership of a given communal resource to any agency (e.g., village wasteland with the state's department of land revenue) were ignored by treating such resources as part of CPRs, because in a *de facto* sense they qualified for such treatment. This approach provided the flexibility needed to cover issues as they emerged during the progress of fieldwork over nearly four years. Consequently, the enquiries initially focussed on the role of CPRs in private resource based farming systems but came to involved vast and varied areas that included CPRs. The study addressed issues of environment and ecology; social organization, poverty and equity;

institutional and technological interventions; rural factionalism and participatory development; grassroots democracy and bureaucratic perceptions; and finally the whole dynamic of rural transformation.

2.3 MIX OF METHODS FROM ANTHROPOLOGY, SOCIOLOGY AND ECONOMICS

The focus of the work was first on understanding different aspects of CPRs as the villagers see them. A key feature of the methodology of field investigations was the combined use of research methods and approaches usually associated with different social science disciplines. In particular, approaches followed by anthropologists and rural sociologists were intensively used for three reasons. Firstly, they helped obtain a better understanding of available oral histories and people's perceptions vis a vis CPRs. Second, due to the primacy of institutional dimensions in CPR issues, anthropological approaches proved to be more helpful. Third, they helped integrate the large number of available records and information with the sociocultural-economic processes at micro and macro levels.

The above approaches were supplemented by methods used for agro-economic investigation that involve recording the quantitative dimensions of CPR issues. Depending on the nature of issues covered (e.g., change in the area of CPRs or seasonal collection of fuel/fodder from CPR plots) and the availability of assistants and cooperators with requisite skills, quantitative data were collected with different frequencies (e.g., ranging from once a year to once a week). Most of the village level assistants in the study had not only witnessed the changes in CPR situation but also participated in the process of change and faced its consequences. However, the key limitation of this approach is that it is much too demanding in terms of workers' personal commitment, their shared concerns, and of course their time and patience. Usual field research conducted in "project mode," i.e., research projects supported by donors, project authorities, etc., have rigid objectives, procedures, timetables, and methods. In contrast the present CPR research had ample flexibility because the researchers were not strictly bound by any pre-given research design except the need to meet some basic conditions such as confinement of the studies to the dry regions of India, covering major soil-rainfall zones within the dry regions, and the identification of complementarities between CPR and PPR (private property resource) based farming systems. ICRISAT's logistic support was always available for the work, but its use was reduced to the minimum by depending on district and village level local facilities. This was in keeping with the useful tradition of anthropological investigations, in which deliberate methodological efforts are made to bridge, eliminate or reduce the gap between researcher and respondents. Moreover, CPR studies involved a number of sensitive issues which could not have been covered through routinely structured surveys.

3. CONTRIBUTIONS MADE BY COMMON PROPERTY RESOURCES (CPRs)

In the context of India's dry region villages, CPRs perform several economic functions. Mainly, these are: contributions to people's employment; income generation; food supply; and asset accumulation (directly or through complementing the private resource based activities). However, being part of the "routine," they are taken for granted and are seldom recognized and recorded. Even more "invisible" are the long-term social and environmental contributions made by CPRs to sustaining life in dry areas.

Table 2 sketches the broad picture of contributions made by various CPRs. They range from direct, visible contributions in terms of supplying physical items, to less visible gains implied by the sustainability of agro-ecological systems.

3.1 QUANTIFICATION OF BENEFITS

Because of monitoring and measurement complexities, a complete quantification of the contributions made by CPRs (as indicated in Table 2) is not easy, although it was attempted in the field. The most relevant information, however, is summarized in Table 3 (see also Jodha 1986) and it documents the large extent of people's dependence on CPRs.

Table 2
CONTRIBUTIONS OF COMMON PROPERTY RESOURCES
TO VILLAGE ECONOMY IN DRY REGIONS OF INDIA[a]

Contributors	CPRs[b]					
	A	B	C	D	E	F
PHYSICAL PRODUCTS:						
Food/Fibre items	X		X	X		
Fodder/fuel/timber, etc.	X	X	X		X	X
Water				X	X	
Manure/silt/space	X	X	X			X
INCOME/EMPLOYMENT GAINS:						
Off-season activities	X				X	X
Drought period sustenance	X	X				X
Additional crop activities			X	X		X
Additional animals	X	X				
Petty trading/handicrafts	X					X
LARGER SOCIAL, ECOLOGICAL GAINS:						
Resource conservation	X	X				
Drainage/recharge of ground water Sustenance of the poor			X	X	X	
Sustainability of farming systems	X	X	X		X	X
Renewable resource supply	X	X	X			
Better micro-climate/environment	X	X		X	X	

a/ Table from Jodha (1985b).

b/ CPRs: A - Community forest; B - Pasture/waste land; C - Pond/tank; D - River/rivulet; E - Watershed drainage/river banks; F - River/tank beds.

Owing to their degradation and reduced productivity, CPRs at present do not offer high returns to their users. Hence, all sections of a rural community are not equally attracted by these gains. Rural poor with limited alternative means of income depend more on the low pay-off options offered by CPRs. Rural rich, i.e., large farmers, indicated by the category "others" in Table 3, depend very little on CPRs.

The proportion of poor households depending on fuel, fodder and food items from CPRs ranged between 84 to 100 percent in different villages. The corresponding figures for rich households, except in very dry villages of Rajasthan, ranged between 10 to 19 percent (Jodha 1986). The recent tendency on the part of rural rich is to acquire CPR land as private property rather than to rely on a share of the meager output from these resources. The intermediate categories of households, not included in Table 3, depend more on CPRs than do the rich.

Table 3 suggests the following inferences:

(i) the rural poor receive the bulk of their fuel supplies and fodder from CPRs;

(ii) CPR product collection is an important source of employment and income, especially during the periods when other opportunities are almost non-existent;

(iii) CPR income, although likely to be under-estimated, accounts for 14 to 23 percent of household income from all other sources in the study villages;

(iv) most importantly, the inclusion of CPR income in total household incomes from other sources, reduces the extent of rural income inequalities, as indicated by lower values of the Gini-coefficient.

Table 3

EXTENT OF PEOPLE'S DEPENDENCE ON COMMON PROPERTY RESOURCES[a]

States (with number of districts and villages) studies	Household categories[b]	CPR's Contribution to Household Supplies, Employment, Income, etc.						
		Fuel supplies[c]	Animal Grazing[d]	Per Household: Employment[e] Days	Per Household: Annual income[f]	CPR-income as proportion[g]	Value of Gini-coefficient of incomes from[h]: all sources	Value of Gini-coefficient of incomes from[h]: all sources excluding CPRs
		(%)	(%)	(No.)	(Rs.)	(%)	(%)	(%)
Andhra Pradesh (1,2)	Poor	84	-	139	534	17	0.41	0.50
	Others	13	-	35	62	1	0.41	0.50
Gujarat (1,2)	Poor	66	82	196	774	18	0.33	0.45
	Others	8	14	80	185	1	0.33	0.45
Karnataka (1,2)	Poor	-	83	185	649	20	-	-
	Others	-	29	34	170	3	-	-
Madhya Pradesh (2,4)	Poor	74	79	183	733	22	0.34	0.44
	Others	32	34	52	386	2	0.34	0.44
Maharashtra (3,6)	Poor	75	69	128	557	14	0.40	0.48
	Others	12	27	43	177	1	0.40	0.48
Rajasthan (2,4)	Poor	71	84	165	770	23	-	-
	Others	23	38	61	413	2	-	-
Tamil Nadu (1,2)	Poor	-	-	137	738	22	-	-
	Others	-	-	31	164	2	-	-

a/ This and all other tables in the paper are based on village/household data from study villages reported by Jodha (1986).

b/ Number of sample household from each village varied from 20 to 36 in different districts. "Poor" are defined to include agricultural laborers and small farm (<2 ha. dryland equivalent) households. "Others" include large farm households only.

c/ Fuel gathered from CPRs as proportion of total fuel used during three seasons covering the whole year.

d/ Animal unit grazing days on CPRs as proportion of total animal unit grazing days.

e/ Total employment through CPR product collection.

f/ Income mainly through CPR product collection. The estimation procedure underestimated the actual income derived from CPRs (Jodha 1986).

g/ CPR income as percent of income from all other sources.

h/ Higher value of Gini coefficient indicates higher degree of income inequalities. Calculations are based on income data for 1983-84 from a panel households covered under ICRISAT's village level studies (Singh et al. 1985). The panel of 40 households from each village included 10 households from each of the categories, namely large, medium and small farm households and labor households.

Map 1

DISTRICTS AND NUMBER OF VILLAGES COVERED BY THE STUDY ON COMMON PROPERTY RESOURCES IN DRY REGIONS OF INDIA

A remarkable finding was that, in the case of rural poor, per worker employment days generated by CPR-based activities were higher than the days of employment on their own farm or on public works under the anti-poverty programs. The potential for self employment and income generation can be further enhanced through development and proper management of CPRs as indicated by villages with better upkeep of CPRs compared to the others.

3.2 CONTRIBUTIONS TO PRIVATE FARMING

The real significance of the CPR-contributions becomes clear when their end uses are examined. This highlights the complementary role of CPRs in private property based farming systems. Table 4 presents some evidence for small and marginal farm households in different areas. Thirty-one to 42 percent of the total own farm inputs used during the pre-sowing to pre-harvest stages of cropping are contributed in cash or kind obtained from CPRs. CPRs contribution during other stages of the cropping season are smaller due to the availability of alternative means, such as wage earnings.

Still greater dependence of private resource-based crop farming on CPRs is revealed by the extent of support that farms receive from CPRs for the sustenance of farm animals. Maintenance of such animals without the CPR facility would have meant the diversion of a substantial proportion (48-55 percent) of crop lands from food and cash crops to fodder crops. The alternative option, i.e., reducing animal numbers to a level sustainable by own fodder/feed resources, would have implied loss of own farm inputs, e.g., draft power (68-76 percent) and farm yard manure (35-43 percent).

Table 4 reveals CPRs' contribution to drought period sustenance of the farm families. If the help received through relief and credit is excluded, 42-57 percent of the total sustenance income

Table 4
CPRs' CONTRIBUTIONS OF PPR-BASED FARMING SYSTEMS[a]

	Items	Range of Values in Different Areas		
(A)	Proportion of cash/kind inflows in total own inputs used during different stages of cropping			
	• Pre-sowing to pre-harvesting	(%)	31-42	
	• Harvest	(%)	11-16	
	• Post harvest	(%)	8-10	
(B)	Potential decline in own resource availability for cropping in the absence of CPRs[b]			
	• Draft power	(%)	68-76	
	• Manure/dung	(%)	35-43	
	• Land area for cash/food crops	(%)	48-55	
	• Crop by product for sale	(%)	84-96	
(C)	CPR contribution to total sustenance income (excluding relief and credit) during[c]			
	• Drought years	(%)	42-57	(68-72)[d]
	• Non-drought years	(%)	14-22	(25-38)

a. Data under section (A) and (B) covering average of two cropping years (1983 and 1984) relate to small and marginal farmers (i.e., those having < 2 ha. dry land equivalent of area). The districts and number of sample households covered are as follows: Mahabubnagar (13), Akola (10), Sholapur (12), Sabarkantha (20), Raisen (18).

b. Procedure for estimating potential decline in own resource supplies (following the non availability of CPRs) was as follows. (i) Average fodder requirement and output of small number of animals currently stall fed for 6 to 8 months a year were estimated. (ii) This average was applied to currently owned animals receiving negligible stall feeding, to estimate their fodder requirement and its implications in terms of transfer of own land area from cash and food crops to fodder crops and reduced marketable surplus of crop by-products. In the absence of above potential adjustments, the implications in terms of reduced animal numbers and consequent decline in draft power and manure supplies were estimated.

c. Data based on studies of drought years and post-drought years conducted in the following districts (with number of sample households), Banaskantha in Gujarat (100), Barmer and Jodhpur, in Rajasthan (144 and 100 respectively), Sholapur in Maharashtra (80). For details see Jodha (1978).

d. Figures in the parentheses indicate percent of village households using CPRs

Table adapted from Jodha 1990b.

during drought years is contributed by cash and kind inflows from CPRs. The corresponding figures for non-drought years (post-drought years) are 14-22 percent. The key inferences relating to CPR-PPR complementarity revealed by Table 4 are as follows (Jodha, 1987b):

(i) Due to the short wet period (planting period) and quantity of manure required for his land, the dry land farmer keeps more animals than could be maintained or fully utilized over the year by his narrow production base. The implied high overhead cost of private crop farming is met through CPRs as a source of fodder and forage.

(ii) Owing to non-co-variability of production flows (and input requirements) of CPR -- use and PPR -- based farming, CPRs help fill in the resource and product gaps faced by private resource based farming.

(iii) Pressure on CPRs is greater when the productivity of PPR based farming (as during the drought years) is low. The same is true in the spatial context when areas with high and low cropping potential are compared (Chambers et al. 1989, Iyengar 1988).

(iv) PPR based farming in the dryland context can be strengthened though revitalization of CPRs.

3.3 COLLECTIVE AND ENVIRONMENTAL GAINS

A number of CPR benefits that accrue to whole villages rather than to the individual households were also recorded for some villages where selected CPRs were still managed well. A few of these benefits are listed: for instance, such villages demonstrated better irrigation practices, (due to better management of river/rivulet beds/banks); had lesser incidence of run-off or drought induced crop-resowing and crop failure (due to better management of watershed through natural vegetation, tamed drainage and soil working); had no drinking water problems (due to collective upkeep of watering points); had dependable water supply from dug wells even during the drought years (due to better soil works and management of watershed and fields in the catchment); had high income generating cottage industries based on CPR products (gum, wild fruits, fiber, etc.); had income (in cash or kind) from CPRs to maintain the village bulls and pay for improved facilities in village school; and had less dependence on government grants and relief. These villages were self-sufficient and produced a surplus of off-season vegetables.

These and a few other less quantifiable gains such as those relating to the environment (e.g., protection of young trees, less unseasonal lopping of trees, etc.) came to light while preparing the village profiles during the field studies. However, it should be noted that not all of the above features relate to the same set of villages. Instead, out of a total of 82 villages covered by the study, there were 33 which had one or more of the above features.

3.4 THE NON-RECOGNITION OF COMMON PROPERTY RESOURCES CONTRIBUTIONS

Despite visible and invisible, short term and long term, individual and collective gains from CPRs, these resources have remained one of the most neglected areas in development planning in India. Whether one looks at the employment and income generation programs, applied nutrition programs, poverty eradication and equity promotion programs, and the resource management and environmental stability programs for the dry regions, no plan documents make explicit reference to CPR contributions and develop an approach to harness them. This is not to say that the government is ignorant about the role of natural resources base in the above listed programs. But public sector interventions treat village community's natural resources merely as bio-physical entities with little concern for the social organization pattern of CPRs and its requirements for designing a strategy to improve performance. Finally, a number of welfare and development interventions (to be discussed later) have had severe negative side effects on CPRs.

4. DEPLETION OF COMMON PROPERTY RESOURCES

Disregard of CPRs and their contributions by welfare and production programs does not only lead to their marginalization as a useful resource, but is also causing their depletion in terms of area shrinkage and productivity decrease. This in turn induces further falls in their pay-off, to be followed by further neglect and degradation. Of the two forms of depletion of CPRs, area shrinkage is relatively easy to observe with the help of written or oral records of village land usage. In contrast, the fall in production from CPRs, although keenly felt by villagers, is difficult to quantify because their productivity has not been recorded in the past.

4.1 DECLINE OF CPR AREAS

Changes in area have been recorded for community pastures, village forests, waste lands and other minor CPRs such as the community threshing grounds, watershed drainages, and fallowed catchments of ponds in all the 82 villages covered by the study. The reference period is 1950-52 when comprehensive land reforms were introduced in the country. The introduction of land reforms initiated changes in the status and management pattern of CPRs. Moreover, being a major event in the memory of villagers, land reforms also provided an important context that facilitated recording of oral history of CPRs.

The 1982-1986 situation of CPRs, when the field work was conducted, was compared with that during 1950-1952. According to Table 5, CPR areas have declined by 31 to 55 percent in the study villages of different states. The impact of this change is clearly visible in terms of both the decline in proportions of CPR lands in total village area and the increase in population pressure on CPRs. Continuation of the decline trends in CPRs has also been recorded by several other studies, subsequent to our own, in different parts of the country (Iyengar 1988, Blaikie et al. 1985, Brara 1987, Chopra et al. 1990).

Table 5
EXTENT AND DECLINE OF CPR AREAS[a]

State (and Number of Districts)	Number of Study Villages	Area of CPRs[b]	CPRs as Proportion of Total Village Area		Decline in the Area of CPRs Since 1950-52	Persons Per 10 ha. of CPR Area	
		1982-84 (ha)	1982-84 (%)	1950-52 (%)	(%)	1951 (No.)	1981 (No.)
Andhra Pradesh (3)	10	827	11	18	42	48	134
Gujarat (3)	15	589	11	19	44	82	238
Karnataka (4)	12	1165	12	20	40	46	117
Madhya Pradesh (3)	14	1435	24	41	41	14	47
Maharashtra (3)	13	918	15	22	31	40	88
Rajasthan (3)	11	1849	16	36	55	13	50
Tamil Nadu (2)	7	412	10	21	50	101	286

a. Table adapted from Jodha (1986), where more disaggregated details are reported.

b. CPRs include community pasture, village forest, waste land, watershed drainage, river and rivulet banks and other common lands. Data indicate average area per village.

The long historical process of privatization of CPR lands in India's dry regions studied had all the key characteristics of such processes identified in other agro-ecological settings, such as the hill area of Azad Kashmir-Pakistan (Cernea 1989). As demonstrated in Cernea's study, the three broad historical stages of the gradual shrinkage of village commonlands were, first, informal partitioning, then incremental appropriation, followed by formal privatization. Comparable processes occurred in India as well, involving a gradual extension of private field borders into adjoining CPR land, outright grabbing of CPR plots by influential village individuals, followed in due course by some legalization by the government. Another form of privatization in India was the distribution of CPRs land as private land by the government (more on this later). Yet another way in which CPR area was curtailed involved acquisition of such lands by the government through its own agencies, such as forest department or contractors, or for using such lands for other public facilities such as the village *panchayat* complex.

4.2 PHYSICAL DEGRADATION OF CPRs

In the absence of recorded benchmark information for assessing degradation or decline in productivity of CPRs over time, a benchmark had to be constructed from oral history and scattered village records. Evidence about continuous decline in productivity and production potential of CPRs, collected by the author during 1982-1986 study, confirms and amplifies the initial findings (see Jodha 1987a, 1990a). This evidence is summarized in Table 6. Findings of other researchers (Iyengar 1988; Brara 1987; Burman 1986) corroborate our conclusion regarding the decreasing production potential of CPRs.

Table 6

SOME INDICATORS OF PHYSICAL DEGRADATION OF CPRs[a]

Indicators of Changed Status and Context for Comparison	States (with number of villages)						
	Andhra Pradesh (3)	Gujarat (4)	Karnataka (2)	Madhya Pradesh (4)	Maharashtra (3)	Rajasthan (4)	Tamil Nadu (2)
CPR - products collected by villagers:[b]							
• In the past (no.)	32	35	40	46	30	27	29
• At present (no.)	9	11	19	22	10	13	8
Per hectare number of trees and shrubs in:							
• Protected CPRs[c]	476	684	662	882	454	517	398
• Unprotected CPRs	195	103	202	215	77	96	83
Number of watering points (ponds) in grazing CPRs:							
• In the past	17	29	20	16	9	48	14
• At present	4	13	4	3	4	11	3
Number of CPR plots where rich vegetation, indicated by their nomenclature, is no more available	--	12	3	6	4	15	--
CPR area used for cattle grazing in the past, currently grazed mainly by sheep/goat (ha)[d]	48	112	95	--	52	175	64

a. Table adapted from Jodha (1990a); based on observation and physical verification of status at the time of field research, compared to the situation in the past as reflected in collected oral and recorded descriptions of CPRs in different villages. The choice of CPRs where plot based data are reported was guided by availability of past information about them.

b. Includes different types of fruits, flowers, leaves, roots, timber, fuel, fodder, etc., in the villages. "Past" indicates the period preceding the 1950s. "Present" indicates the early 1980s.

c. Protected CPRs were the areas (called "oran") where for religious reasons live trees and shrubs are not cut. The situation of CPR plots (numbering between 2 to 4 in different areas) was compared with other bordering plots of CPRs which were not protected by any religious or other sanctions.

d. Relates to area covered by specific plots, traditionally used for grazing high productivity animals (e.g., cattle in milk, working bullocks or horses of feudal landlords). Because of the commons' depletion, such animals are no more grazed there.

A drastic decline in the number of products on the remaining CPR lands, following the disappearance of a number of plant and tree species which villagers used to gather from the commons in the past (i.e., before the early 1950s), is a major indicator of environmental degradation of CPRs. The local (vernacular) names of certain plots indicated that they were covered by specific vegetation in the past. At present hardly any of those species grow there. Similarly, a number of selected CPR plots that were traditionally used for grazing more productive animals, such as lactating cattle, working bullocks, etc., are no longer able to support these animals. With their forage potential depleted and vegetative composition changed, they are now grazed by sheep and goats instead of cattle. The number of watering points, an important component of common grazing lands, has also declined.

The difference in the number of species found on protected and unprotected CPRs is an important indicator of vegetative degradation and associated resource depletion. Certain CPR areas are protected through religious sanctions against the removal of live trees, shrubs, etc. We found that the per hectare number of trees and shrubs was 3 to 6 times higher in protected CPRs compared to unprotected ones (Table 6).

An important indicator of reduced productivity of CPRs is when local people must spend greater time and travel longer distances to collect the same or a lesser quantity of CPR products today as compared to the past. Similarly, in the past the whole village community used CPRs; at present, as indicated earlier, it is mainly the poorer households, with few alternative options, that try to meet their needs from these meager resources.

4.3 WEAKENED SOCIAL ORGANIZATION AND THE INCREASE IN PAUPERIZATION

The physical degradation of CPRs has been paralleled by the gradual erosion of the social arrangements that used to maintain CPRs as an asset-pool available to all entitled beneficiaries. In particular, the local management of these resources has been weakened, meaning that village-based authority systems, consensual rules of contribution, and penalties for abusers do not operate any more as they did in the past. For instance, the inability to enforce obligations of CPR users (in terms of grazing tax or compulsory labor input for trenching, fencing, etc.) is a cause of worsening maintenance and of transformation of CPRs into *de facto* open access. Physical degradation and weakened social organization are linked into a reciprocal cause-effect interaction.

The slackening or even complete abolition of some traditional formal/informal management practices for CPRs are signaled by many researchers, in addition to our own findings (see Chambers et al. 1989; Burman 1986; Singh 1986; Arnold and Stewart 1989). In Table 7 we have captured some specific aspects of this multisided process -- namely, the discontinuation of several social patterns that constituted a part-and-parcel of traditional management systems over CPRs. The table demonstrates that in most states less than a tenth of the villages currently follow the social patterns under which CPRs used to function in the past.

The current status of CPRs is a defining characteristic of rural poverty in dry areas. Depletion of CPRs and the entailed decline in access to bio-mass indicates pauperization (Chambers et al. 1989) because the roles of CPRs, reflected in tables 1 and 2, have become less feasible. However, the pauperization process involves more than this and has several long-term consequences.

Table 7
SOME INDICATIONS OF CHANGES IN THE MANAGEMENT OF CPRs[a]

State (with Number of Villages)	Number of Villages Pursuing the Following Measures: Formal/Informal Regulations on CPR Use[b]		Formal/Informal Taxes/Levis on CPR Use[d]		Users' Formal/Informal Obligation Towards Upkeep of CPR[e]	
	In the Past[c]	At Present	In the Past	At Present	In the Past	At Present
Andhra Pradesh (10)	10	--[f]	7	--	8	--
Gujarat (15)	15	2	8	--	11	2
Karnataka (12)	12	2	9	--	12	3
Madhya Pradesh (14)	14	2	10	--	14	3
Maharashtra (13)	11	1	6	--	10	1
Rajasthan (11)	11	1	11	--	11	2
Tamil Nadu (7)	7	--	4	--	7	1

a. Table adapted from Jodha (1990a).

b. Measures such as regulated/rotational grazing, seasonal restrictions on use of CPRs, provision of CPR watchmen, etc.

c. "Past" stands for the period prior to the 1950s, present stands for the early 1980s.

d. Measures such as grazing taxes, levies, and penalties for violation of regulations on use of CPRs. See Jodha (1985a) for a descriptive account.

e. Measures such as contribution towards desilting of watering points, fencing, trenching, protection of CPRs, etc.

f. (-) indicates nil.

First, the transfer of submarginal CPR lands to crop cultivation through their privatization is tantamount to a step towards long-term unsustainability of land based activities in dry regions (Jodha 1988b, 1989b and 1991).

Second, reduced production and income options entail increased scarcity and stress for those who depend on CPRs. The longer time and distance involved in collecting the same or lesser quantities of CPR products and the more reduced effective period (months) of sustained grazing offered by CPRs today, as compared to the past, are just two of the several examples of this phenomenon.

Third, despite the inferior options available from CPRs, the rural poor continue to depend on them. This is because the opportunity cost of the poor's labor to harness the inferior options is still lower. Hence, the progressive decline in the value of CPR products, accompanied by an equally increasing number of people relying on them for sustenance, is a definite indicator of increasing poverty. The whole process remains invisible, but it implies a situation where a community silently eats away its permanent asset. Since the poor are sustained by CPRs without any direct and visible burden on the public exchequer (through community subsidy or development assistance), not many would realize that the loss of CPRs may prove costlier than any alternative means to help the poor.

The final consequence of the vicious circle involving poverty and CPR degradation is reflected in the elimination or disruption of vital bio-physical processes (e.g., regeneration, nutrient and moisture flows, etc.), which contribute to the maintenance of the physical productivity of natural resources in dry regions (Jodha, 1991) even outside the areas under a commons regime.

5. THE CAUSES OF COMMON PROPERTY RESOURCES' DECLINE

Which processes account causally for this decline in CPRs? How do these processes occur and unfold?

The decline in area, productivity, and upkeep of CPRs has been a part of the scenario in most developing countries where these resources continue to be important (Sanford 1983). The recent literature on the subject attributes these changes to population growth, market forces, public sector interventions, technological changes and environmental stress (e.g., drought), (Runge 1981; Repetto and Holmes 1984; Ciriacy - Wantrup and Bishop 1975; Bromley and Chapagain 1984; Bromley and Cernea 1989). Figure 1 sketches the process through which these factors, individually or jointly, contribute to the decline and depletion of CPRs. These factors influence the informal or formal norms and arrangements governing people's approach to CPRs. These norms and arrangements can alter with changes in the perceptions and needs of the community (Magrath 1986). These changes in turn are reflected through public policies and interventions and local communities' responses to them.

5.1 PUBLIC SECTOR INTERVENTIONS AFFECTING CPRs

Public policies and programs influencing CPRs can be grouped under three categories, namely: (i) those affecting the area of CPRs; (ii) those relating to products and productivity of CPRs; and (iii) those influencing the management, usage and upkeep of CPRs. There also are public sector measures which fall under more than one of the above categories.

Figure 1

PROCESS OF DEPLETION OF COMMON PROPERTY RESOURCES IN THE DRY REGIONS OF INDIA

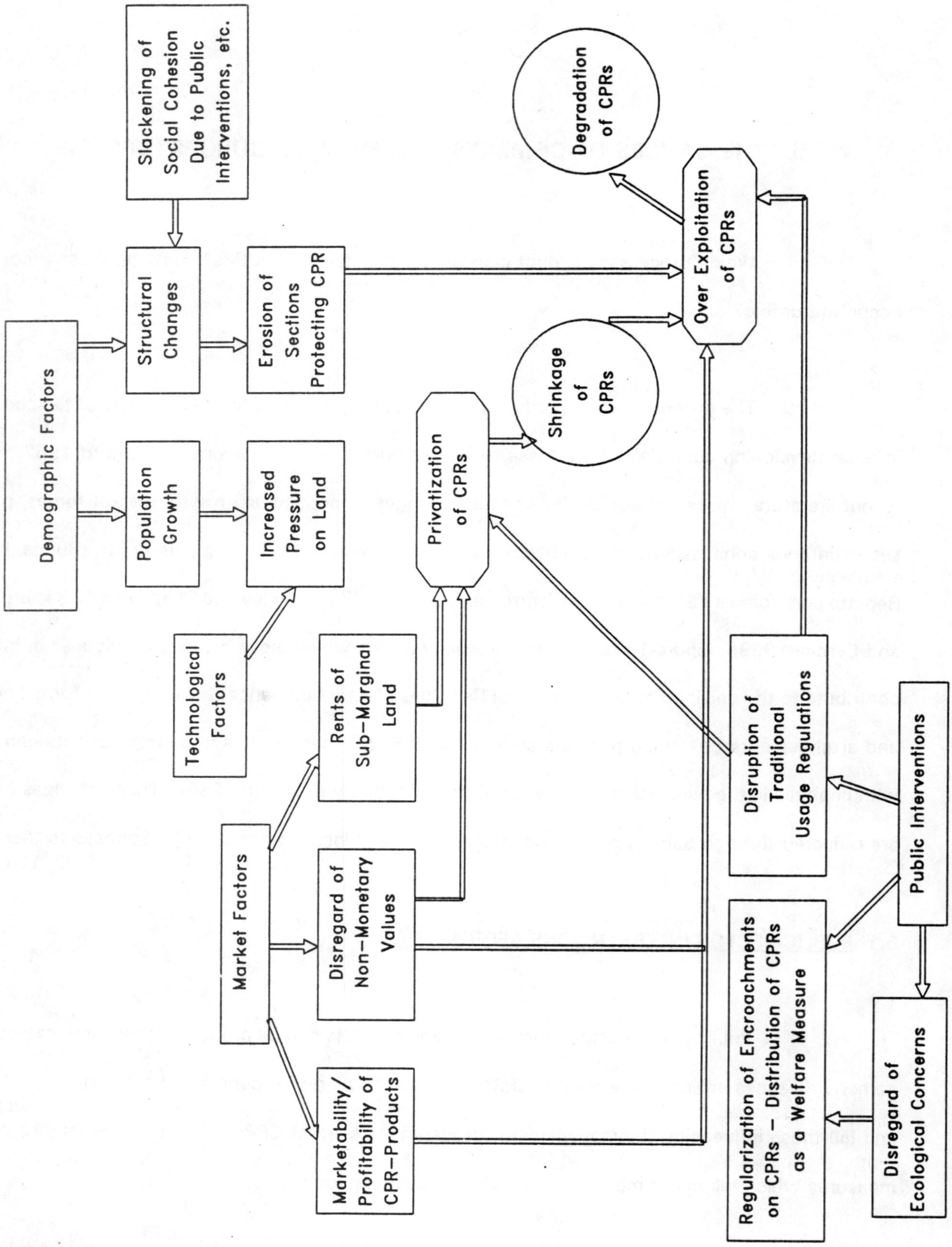

Area Shrinkage. As revealed by Table 5, large scale privatization of CPRs has led to a decline in their extent in all the areas studied. This change is closely associated with the government's land distribution policies, beginning with the introduction of land reforms in the early 1950s and continued up to the present, which have encouraged the privatization of CPRs. Practically all the programs designed to provide land to specific beneficiaries, mainly landless people, have resulted in the curtailment of CPRs. Having failed to acquire land for redistribution through land ceiling laws (Ladejinsky 1972) or through voluntary donation under movements like Bhoodan, (voluntary donation of land by private land owners), the curtailment of CPR lands was found to be the easiest option. Privatization was carried out either through (i) the formal distribution of commons land to landless and other groups under different welfare or development schemes, or through (ii) the legalization of illegal grabbing of CPR lands by people. Both steps entailed increased pressure on the remaining CPRs.

Under the rhetorical cover of helping the poor, the privatization of CPRs brought more land to the already better off households. According to Table 8, the proportion of poor households among recipients of CPR lands was generally higher in all the villages studied. However, the amount of land they received was much lower than that of the other social groups. On average, the poor received barely more than one hectare per household. The corresponding area received by "others" ranged between 2 to 3 hectares. The last column of Table 8 reveals that those who already had relatively more land also received more of the privatized CPR land.

Furthermore, as revealed by detailed enquiry, poor households in all but one area were soon dispossessed of 23 to 45 percent of the land received. The reasons included lack of complementary resources to develop and use the land. Additionally, land quality was too poor to sustain annual cropping (Jodha 1986).

Table 8

DISTRIBUTION OF PRIVATIZED CPR LANDS TO DIFFERENT HOUSEHOLD GROUPS[a]

State (with Number of Villages)	Total Land Given (ha)	Total Household Receiving Land (No.)	Share of Poor[b] in (2) (%)	Proportion of Poor in (3) (%)	Per Household Land Received by		Average Land Size After Receiving New Land	
					Poor (ha)	Others[c] (ha)	Poor (ha)	Others (ha)
1	2	3	4	5	6	7	8	9
Andhra Pradesh (6)	493	401	50	74	1.0	2.1	1.6	5.0
Gujarat (8)	287	166	20	45	1.0	2.6	1.8	9.4
Karnataka (9)	362	203	43	65	1.3	3.0	2.2	8.0
Madhya Pradesh (10)	358	204	42	62	1.2	3.2	2.5	9.5
Maharashtra (8)	316	227	38	53	1.1	1.9	2.0	6.2
Rajasthan (7)	635	426	22	36	1.2	3.2	1.9	7.2
Tamil Nadu (7)	447	272	49	66	1.0	1.5	1.9	6.7

a. Table adapted from Jodha (1986). Number of districts covered by the table are 3 in each of the States except Andhra Pradesh and Tamil Nadu where 2 districts each were covered.

b. "Poor" includes agricultural laborers and small farm (<2 ha of dry land equivalent) households.

c. "Others" in this table, unlike other tables, includes both medium and large farm households.

Thus, the government's policies to help the rural poor through land distribution did not work as intended. It is quite doubtful whether poor people's collective loss through reduced CPRs has been compensated by their individual ownership of ex-CPR lands.

<u>Productivity Decline</u>. The policies and programs for raising the productivity of CPRs adopted since the early 1950s generally lacked an in-depth perspective on CPRs, particularly an understanding of what it takes to strengthen their social organization and how the involved social actors behave. For instance, even when the names of various programs refer to community, (e.g., rehabilitation of "community forest" or "community pastures"), they are often treated as state run activities. Such programs are conceived as top-down measures relating to physical resources located in the villages, implemented by administrative cum legal procedures and to be sustained by state subsidies with very little involvement of village communities. A typical case in point are the many projects during the 1980s financing so called "community woodlots" on land plots usually carved out from the village commons. Cernea (1991) has summarized evidence about the failure of most government and Bank supported "community woodlot" schemes in India in the 1980s, which have not relied on appropriate social actors and ended up as administratively led interventions with little results other than diminishing the CPR lands left available to the poorest people.

Another feature of the initiatives for productivity raising or CPRs is the almost exclusive focus on production technology (Gupta 1987; Shankarnaryana and Kalla 1985; Jodha 1988b). These programs emphasize science and technology rather than community involvement and user perspectives. Hence, one comes across long inventories of technically assessed species of trees and grasses, methods for reseeding rangelands and reforesting wastelands, plant establishment and thinning techniques, and a variety of other sylvicultural or agrostological recommendations for community lands. However, there is little in terms of the institutional ability of the above measures to raise productivity on the CPRs involved. Moreover, to establish and demonstrate the viability of technological measures, in several cases community lands are alienated from the people and transferred to pilot projects (Chambers et al. 1989).

Even the donor-supported initiatives for raising productivity of CPRs often share similar features. For instance as part of a World Bank supported project (during early 1970s) called "drought proofing of drought prone areas", pasture development was made an important activity in the districts of Nagaur and Jodhpur (Rajasthan). The present author visited nearly a dozen of CPR-units (called Jod, Beed, etc.) in these districts at two points in time. The project provided for fencing, new plantations and soil improvement works on the above plots, and included a budget for the purpose of providing watchmen and facilities for the *panchayats*. The key decision makers about project activities were district officials from the soil conservation, planning and statistics departments, important officials of the district and village *panchayats*, and a few village influentials who managed to present their private land as CPRs in order to capture benefits from the project. Villagers in general were unhappy with the project as it not only reduced their usable resources but it provided no chance for their complaints and views. Shortly after the end of the project (during the second visit of the author), in 8 out of 13 cases, all the physical and institutional arrangements provided by the project had disappeared. Of the remaining five cases (that showed a visible impact from the project), three belonged to influential individuals as their private grazing cum fodder collection fields. The above illustration has some commonalities with the unsuccessful schemes in different parts of Africa described by Bromley and Cernea (1989).

One serious consequence of productivity raising efforts initiated without sufficient concern for the users' perspective is the virtual conversion of CPR lands into fields for commercial production, as witnessed in a number of social forestry projects (Chambers et al. 1989, Arnold and

Stewart 1989, and Gupta 1987). In the process, most of the functions of CPRs referred to in Table 2 are sacrificed.

The more productive CPRs are faced with yet another problem -- the state's attempts to grab such resources. Directly or through contractors, the state acquires a monopoly on the collection or marketing of CPR products from these resources (Jodha 1985b, Chambers et al. 1989). This deprives the village communities or specific groups from having the full benefit of high productivity CPRs. The villagers' protests have sometimes produced prolonged litigation, but more often, facing the risk of losing such resources, villagers adopt more desperate strategies and overexploit such resources whenever opportunity comes.

Weakened Social Organization and Self-Management. As mentioned earlier, the traditional management systems for CPRs, (involving usage regulation, enforcement of users' obligations, and investments for conservation and development) have practically disappeared. We see this as a side effect of certain institutional reforms, such as the introduction of land reforms and of the new village *panchayat* system (elected village councils). The former led to the abolition of a number of levies and taxes on CPR users (Jodha 1985a). The latter undermined the traditional informal authority of village elders and replaced the formal authority of feudal landlords in some areas, but *panchayats* have failed to assume effective responsibility for the CPRs. Despite their legal powers, village *panchayats* are generally unable to enforce any regulation about CPRs.

Panchayats' dependence on community votes, compelling them to avoid unpopular steps like enforcing CPR-user obligations, and their domination by village leaders with little personal interest in CPRs, make the new institutions ineffective (Jodha 1985a, Gupta 1987 and Arnold and Stewart 1989). However, *panchayats* rarely miss any opportunity to seek government grants in the name of CPRs. Default on the part of *panchayats* has thus played a decisive role in converting CPRs into open access resources and in what follows in terms of the tragedy of "open access resource" (Bromley and Cernea, 1989). The exceptions are the cases where the village elders still exercise informal authority over CPRs (Brara 1987).

Furthermore, traditional consensual arrangements and informal systems of social sanctions relating to the use and maintenance of CPRs have been replaced by un-enforceable legal and administrative measures. This has marginalized the people's initiatives and alienated them from CPRs. It has also encouraged dependence on government grants or relief rather than mobilize local resources (as in the past) for the upkeep of CPRs.

Ironically, village *panchayats*, the small scale replica of the state, and the formal source of (unenforceable) authority at the village level, continue to be the focal point of development interventions which are externally conceived. Despite being part of the village, in most cases the *panchayats* are less sensitive to village realities (including declining CPRs) and more responsive to signals (or rather temptations) from above. No wonder that in such cases, people are seeking alternative organizations (e.g., user groups, the involvement of NGOs) to manage community resources.

Side Effects of Other Developments. Besides such public interventions directly related to CPRs, there are other components of general rural development strategies that affect CPRs through their own negative side effects. A few examples will clarify this point.

The government subsidized process of tractorization has led to a rapid conversion of submarginal CPR lands into croplands (Jodha 1974, 1985a). Increased monetization and commercialization of rural areas has adversely affected people's attitude to CPRs (Jodha 1985b, 1988a). Improved accessibility and market integration of hitherto isolated, fragile areas into the main stream economy have also led to over exploitation of CPRs (Jodha 1985a, 1985b). As mentioned earlier, programs like social forestry have changed the composition of products and poor people's access to CPRs (Chambers et al. 1989; Cernea 1991). The argument here is not against the development of rural areas but against the underlying designs which failed to integrate CPRs into the development processes.

5.2 ROLE OF DONOR AGENCIES

In general, the decline of CPRs can be attributed to donor agencies only indirectly, in terms of their support to state policies that adversely affected CPRs. On the face of it, this may seem paradoxical since donors operate through national agencies and the latter alone should be held responsible for neglect of CPRs.

However, in view of the evidence about donor's insistence on substantial amendments in the structure and contents of different rural development projects, the above reasoning does not help. The preconditions for several aid programs, such as economic restructuring, environmental safety provisions, and in some cases even insistence on conditions relating to the choice of experts and source of material supplies for the projects, would bear this out. Donor supported resource-centered programs, such as the Drought Proofing of Drought Prone Areas or Social Forestry Projects in India, as well as agricultural research projects, are cases in which donors could have helped shape an in-depth concern for protecting the CPRs for their economic and environmental benefits. However, there too a CPR perspective has largely been missing in the donors' resource centered research strategies.

The disregard of CPR concerns by donors can be attributed to their operational style. First, since in the context of specific projects donors tend to operate on borrowed perspectives (i.e., perspectives of local agencies acceptable to the donors), they would rarely go beyond what their national counterparts would suggest. Second, even when the donors use their own perspectives, the latter are also usually uninformed about the institutional dynamics of CPRs. Third, even when the donors have a deep understanding of the issues or have the desire to incorporate such issues in the projects, their appraisal missions or feasibility study groups operate under time constraints too severe to incorporate them meaningfully in the projects. Finally, the CPR issues (as will be indicated shortly) have several micro-level dimensions. They are likely to be overlooked in broad-based interventions. Interventions need to be fairly location-specific and much smaller in scale, but this may not fit with the donors' operational style. Consequently, relevant and potentially effective initiatives (e.g., as some of those operated by NGOs) may not prove attractive to the donors due to the "economies of scale" argument for not handling small scale interventions. A significant change, however, in the perspective of a major donor like the World Bank regarding common property matters was expressed in the Bank's policy paper for the forest sector (World Bank 1991).

5.3 NON-UNIFORM IMPACT OF PUBLIC INTERVENTIONS

An important qualification to the above discussion on CPRs and public interventions is that it provides an overly-general picture. In practice, the impact of public policies and programs is not uniform everywhere. Depending on local circumstances, including ratios of people to land and the local communities' resilience against changes forced from outside, actual impact varies a great deal. This is partly indicated by the inter-village differences in the decline of CPR areas even within the same district, for which the public policies influencing CPR were the same. Table 9 illustrates this by

Table 9

RANGE OF INTER-VILLAGE DIFFERENCES IN THE EXTENT AND DECLINE OF CPR AREA[a]

State (with Number of Village)	Range of CPR Area as Proportion of Total Village Area in:		Range of Decline in the Area of CPRs:
	1950-52 (%)	1982-84 (%)	1950-52 to 1982-84 (%)
Andhra Pradesh (10)	9-10	5-20	25-56
Gujarat (15)	7-31	2-23	21-69
Karnataka (12)	6-36	4-30	15-50
Madhya Pradesh (14)	29-69	19-47	14-51
Maharashtra (13)	8-43	6-34	14-52
Rajasthan (11)	20-49	8-26	17-71
Tamil Nadu (7)	7-39	5-23	21-65

a. Table adapted from Jodha (1986), based on field work and village records.

presenting inter-village difference in terms of: (i) CPRs area as proportion of total village area during 1950-52 as well as 1982-84 and (ii) percentage decline in CPR area during the above period. Differences in village level impacts of uniform public policies result also from the fact that in the past the proportion of CPRs was not similar in all villages. Moreover, villagers may take varied approaches to different kinds of resources under a commons regime within the same villages.

Other factors influencing CPRs are grouped under: (i) demographic factors (ii) ecological factors, and (iii) market related factors. We will examine their impact only in terms of the decline of CPR areas, for want of sufficient data on other aspects. However, in most cases, there is considerable parallelism between the trends relating to decline in area, productivity and the social organization of CPRs.

5.4 OTHER FACTORS: DEMOGRAPHY, ECOLOGY, MARKET

The specific variables considered for the above three categories of factors influencing CPR areas are as follows. Demographic factors include total size and density of village population; number of households; and growth of population during 1951-1981. Qualitative characteristics of village populations (such as occupational shifts, degree of factionalism and socioeconomic differentiation), are also considered.

The ecological factors include variables such as: area of village (as size of village is often negatively associated with the harshness and marginality of agro-climatic environment); extent of submarginal lands (e.g., low fertility, gravely, sandy, woody lands with undulating topography and some incidence of salinity, water logging, etc.), that are usually kept as CPRs; predominance of extensive pattern of land use reflected by importance of livestock farming, and so on.

Market related factors include distance from the market center; proportion of cash crops in total cropped area; and extent of communication facilities facilitating the market orientation of agriculture. Analysis of village level data (both through bi-variate tabulation and regression), was attempted to detect associations between the above variables and decline of CPR area (Jodha 1987a, 1988a, 1990a).

The broad picture revealed by the analysis is as follows (Table 10).

(i) In smaller and isolated villages, where traditional social sanctions are still respected, the decline of CPR area is less. Transaction costs of enforcing social discipline regarding CPRs are lower in such cases. It is easier to organize "user groups" and group action for CPRs in such a situation as shown by the experience of different NGOs.

(ii) Protection of CPR area is better in the villages relatively further from market-centers, where market forces are less effective in eroding traditional values vis a vis CPRs.

(iii) In smaller and isolated villages (often located in bio-physically less favorable environments) ecological requirements favoring the retention and protection of CPRs are stronger.

(iv) The decline of CPRs is less in the villages with smaller initial CPRs, where communities have fuller knowledge and an active concern about their common resources. Informal, social guarding of CPRs is easier in such areas.

A further analysis was attempted of the association between qualitative features of village populations, and the status of CPRs. Groups of villages with highest and lowest values of specific demographic characteristics (e.g., factionalism, occupational shifts, etc.) were compared with respect to the decline in their CPR area. Details are presented in Table 11, summarized below, showing that the decline in CPR areas is lower in the villages with the following characteristics:

(i) Fewer recent occupational changes (i.e., shift from handicrafts, caste services, etc., to cultivation), implying lesser increase in the demand for conversion of CPR lands into privately cropped lands;

(ii) Lower degree of commercialization (implying less erosion of social sanctions and informal arrangements protecting CPRs);

(iii) Greater degree of social cohesion, conducive to protection of CPRs;

(iv) Lower socioeconomic differentiation (ensuring equity of access and benefits from CPRs, equal stake in the maintenance of CPR and less); private appropriation of resources belonging to the commons.

(v) Less dependence on state patronage for resource transfers to village (implying lesser opportunity for interference in village affairs from above, including for privatization of CPRs as part of populist programs).

Understanding these village level factors and changes helps explain the inter-village differences in the status and management of CPRs. Public interventions pursuing the improved management of natural resources can greatly benefit from the lessons offered by such understanding.

Table 10
TRENDS IN THE STATUS AND CHANGES OF CPR AREA AND ASSOCIATED DEMOGRAPHIC, ECOLOGICAL AND MARKET FACTORS[a]

Attributes of Villages	Relative Position of CPRs			
	Extent of CPR Area (1950-52)		Decline in CPR Area 1950-52 to 1982-84	
	Higher	Lower	Higher	Lower
Demographic Factors:				
Higher population		X		
Greater number of households		X	X	
Higher population increase			X	
Ecological Factors:				
Larger area of village	X		X	
Larger extent of submarginal lands	X		X	
Larger initial area of CPRs			X	
Greater importance of livestock	X			X
Market Related Factors:				
Greater distance from market center	X			X

a. Based on comparison of groups of villages in each state having highest and lowest extent of CPRs, (1950-52) and those having highest and lowest decline of CPRs (1950-52 to 1982-84). For details see Jodha (1990a).

Table 11

DECLINE OF CPR AREA IN THE VILLAGES DIFFERENTIATED BY QUALITATIVE CHANGES IN THEIR POPULATION (1950-52 to 1982-84)

	Changes in Demographic Characteristics	Villages Covered (No.)	Decline in Area of CPRs (%)
A.	*Occupational Change*: Proportion of household who newly shifted to agriculture		
	Higher[a]	27	37
	Lower	21	12
B.	*Degree of Commercialization*:		
	Higher[b]	31	44
	Lower	28	18
C.	*Factionalism, Group Dynamics*:		
	Higher[c]	30	28
	Lower	26	14
D.	*Socioeconomic Differentiation*:		
	Higher[d]	28	42
	Lower	32	15
E.	*Dependence on State Patronage*:		
	Higher[e]	25	60
	Lower	27	16

a. Table adopted from Jodha (1988a). Households that shifted away from traditional caste occupation and became cultivators. Their proportion to total households in the village ranged from 15 to 20 percent and 2 to 5 percent respectively in the villages with "higher" and "lower" occupational shifts.

b. Accessibility to market and related facilities are used as proxy for commercialization. Better accessibility is broadly defined to include the situation of villages having market center within 2 km of distance, availability of more than five shops in the village, regular operation of town based trader or his agent in the village, year round bus service, etc. On the basis of presence or absence of these attributes villages are grouped as those having a "higher" or "lower" degree of commercialization.

c. "Higher" factionalism means presence of two or more factions in village with vast differences in their strength and political patronage from the above. Villages with "lower" factionalism lacked these features. They had factions of equal strength to be able to control each other.

d. Differentiation reflected by values of Gini-coefficient of owned lands holdings, which ranged from 0.63 to 0.75 and 0.34 to 0.40 in the villages with "higher" and "lower" socioeconomic differentiation respectively.

e. Villages which had officially sponsored land (Patta) distribution more than twice during last ten years, had 100 percent dependence on state grant for CPR improvement, are included into "higher" group. The villages with "lower" patronage did not have these attributes.

6. VILLAGE STRATEGIES FOR COPING WITH CHANGING CPRs

Rural communities, operating under the influence of public interventions or pressures generated internally (e.g., though population growth) have contributed to the decline of CPRs at the village level. In the process they have also evolved their own strategies to cope with the changing CPR situation. The focus of such strategies is the maximization of private gains from the worsening status of CPRs. This does not exclude small initiatives directed to protection and rehabilitation of CPRs in some cases.

Since the extent and type of private gains extracted from rapidly declining CPRs are very much related to the capacities and needs of individual families, adaptation strategies are shaped accordingly. Hence, one can notice differences in the responses of rural rich and rural poor towards the changing situation of CPRs. Some responses may be common to both. For instance, both rich and poor attempt to grab CPR lands, despite their different likelihoods of success (Jodha 1986). Table 12 summarizes some relevant aspects of response strategies adopted by different groups in the study villages.

Table 12
PEOPLE'S ADAPTATIONS TO CHANGING SITUATION OF CPRs[a]

Measures Adopted by Different Groups in the Face of Decline in Area, Productivity and Management Systems of CPRs		
Rural Rich	Rural Poor	Rural Community (General)
Withdrawal from CPRs as users of products: (Opportunity cost of labor higher than CPR product value)	*Using of CPRs as an important source of sustenance* Complementarity of CPR-PPR based activities	*Acceptance of CPRs as open access resources*: over-exploitation without users' obligations, regulations
Increased reliance on alternative options • Own bio-mass supplies; (stall feeding, etc.) • Non-renewable/external resources (e.g., replacing stone fencing for thorn fencing, wooden tires for carts, iron tools for local wooden ones	*Acceptance of inferior options* • Opportunity cost of labor lower than value of products of degraded CPRs	*Selective approach to specific CPR units*: despite general neglect of CPRs, concern for some units
Private squeeze on CPRs as assets • Grabbing CPR lands • Preventing others using seasonal CPRs (private crop lands during off-season)	*Measures reflecting desperation* • Premature harvesting of CPR products • Removal of roots/base of products • Over-crowding and over-exploitation of CPRs • Use of hitherto unusable inferior products	*Focus on "other" uses of CPRS*: Item in seeking government subsidy/relief, in running factional quarrels, in populist programs, etc.
Approach to CPR management • Indifference to decline of CPRs • As rural influential party to non-functioning legal and administrative superstructure for community resources		*Party to non-operating legal and administrative measures*: acceptance of external impositions without protest, etc.
		Structural changes/focus on alternative sources • Changes in livestock composition (replacing cattle by sheep/goat, etc.) • Agro-forestry initiative (revival of indigenous agro-forestry, etc.)

a. Based on observations and changes recorded during the field work (1982-85). For elaboration and evidence see, Jodha (1989a), Ayenger (1988), Brara (1987), Arnold and Stewart (1989), Chambers et al. (1989).

6.1 THE RURAL RICH AND CHANGING CPRs

As observed during the field work and corroborated by other evidence, the dominant responses of the rural rich (e.g., large farmers) to the changing situation of CPRs include the following:

(i) Withdrawal from CPRs as users of CPR products since their opportunity cost of labor for collecting/using CPR products is higher than the value of CPR products (Jodha 1986).

(ii) Increased reliance on alternative options (Jodha 1986, 1988b, Arnold and Stewart 1989). Alternatives include: own supplies of biomass, substitution of renewable CPR products by non-renewables and/or external products (e.g., stone fencing for thorn fencing, or rubber tire for wooden tires for bullock carts, iron tools for locally made wooden ones).

(iii) Private squeeze on CPRs assets, as reflected in the tendency to appropriate CPR lands, to prevent others from using their private land during off-season (i.e., seasonal CPRs), and to enrich their own soil by mining silt and top soil from CPR lands and bringing it on private fields (Jodha 1986, 1988b, Iyengar 1988, Brara 1987).

(iv) Indifference to the management of CPRs, despite their influence and ability to use legal cum administrative structures and public funds (grants/subsidies) available for rehabilitation of CPRs (Jodha 1989a, Chambers et al. 1989, Arnold and Stewart 1989).

Perpetuation of the above responses would mean a further decline in CPRs and will ultimately make the resources under a commons regime irrelevant for the rural rich.

6.2 THE RURAL POOR AND CHANGING CPRs

Depending on their capacity, poor households also attempt some of the practices adopted by the rural rich. However, their specific responses include:

(i) Use of CPRs as an important source of sustenance and attempt to maximize complementarity between CPRs and PPRs.

(ii) Ready acceptance of increasingly inferior options offered by CPRs. This is because they lack alternative options and because in most cases their poverty lowers the opportunity cost of their labor.

(iii) Resort to measures manifesting a high degree of desperation. Examples are: increased frequency and unseasonal lopping of trees and pre-mature harvest (collection) of CPR products, reducing seed formation and regeneration possibilities; removal of plant/bush roots (the very basis of CPR products); use of hitherto discarded (inferior) products with negative side effects on the health of users; and over crowding and over exploitation of CPRs (Jodha 1985b, 1988b, and Brara 1987).

The consequence of these trends will be further environmental degradation at the village level and rapid decline of whatever cushion rural poor have through CPRs.

6.3 CHANGING CPRs AND THE RURAL COMMUNITY

Responses against the changing CPR situation adopted by different village groups are reflected at the whole community level. They include:

(i) General acceptance of CPRs as open access resources, following the abolition or disintegration of traditional usage regulations. This is reflected in a complete absence of users' obligations and a consequent over-exploitation of CPRs, as well as in the failure to question the non-functional legal and administrative measures relating to CPRs (Jodha 1988b, 1989a; Singh 1986; Roy Buran 1986; Brara 1987; Blaikie et al. 1986; Odell 1982; Gupta 1986; Bromley and Cernea 1989; and Arnold and Stewart 1989).

(ii) Focus on alternative uses or rather misuses of CPRs, as reflected by: treating CPRs as an issue in factional disputes, projecting CPRs as an item to secure government subsidies/grants for village panchayats, using commons lands for the distribution of political patronage (Jodha 1989a).

(iii) Structural changes such as changes in the composition of livestock species (Table 13) or in revival of agro-forestry (Jodha 1985a, 1988b, 1989b).

(iv) A general neglect of CPRs, with selective management approaches for specific resource types and units (as revealed by Table 14).

The last two categories of community responses to the changing CPR -- situation are elaborated further.

6.4 CHANGES IN THE COMPOSITION OF LIVESTOCK

The CPR decline forces significant adjustments in the livestock sector of the rural economy. Reduced grazing space and depletion of forage potential have made it difficult to productively maintain large numbers of animals. Detailed studies based on data at two points of time in the villages of Rajasthan (Jodha 1985a) indicated both reduction in the size and changes in the composition of animal holdings. Inquiries in other areas confirmed similar trends. According to Table 13, the number of bullocks in the sample households has declined by 19 to 42 percent in different areas during 1982-84 as compared to 1950-52.

What accounts for this trend, in addition to the increased degree of mechanization in certain areas, is the high overhead cost of maintaining bullocks. Using bullocks for only 3-4 months and feeding them for the whole year without CPR support is difficult. The number of cows also declined, for similar reasons. In dry areas, owing to droughts and frequent miscarriages, the cows' prolonged unproductivity period often exceeds their lactation period (Vyas and Jodha 1974). Maintaining unproductive animals without CPR support is difficult. Moreover, the high cost of increased stall feeding favored buffalo keeping against cows, in the context of milk pricing based on amount of fat in milk.

Table 13
STRUCTURAL CHANGES IN LIVESTOCK POPULATION
IN RESPONSE TO DECLINE OF CPRs[a]

State (with Number of Villages and Sample Households)	% Changes (+ or -) in the Number of Animals in 1982-84 Compared to 1950-52[a]			
	Bullock	Cow	Buffalo	Sheep and Goat
Andhra Pradesh (2,38)	- 21	- 18	+ 4	+ 23
Gujarat (4,68)	- 30	- 26	+ 20	+ 19
Karnataka (2,40)	- 22	- 19	+ 9	+ 22
Madhya Pradesh (4,80)	- 16	- 18	+ 12	+ 19
Maharashtra (4,82)	- 31	- 19	+ 12	+ 32
Rajasthan (6,115)	- 42 -(63)[b]	- 35	+ 14	+ 38
Tamil Nadu (2,30)	- 19	- 14	+ 9	+ 21

a. Based on current status and oral history of animal holdings (in 1950-52) of sample households recorded during the field work during 1982-1985. Data for the past adjusted for division of families, etc.

b. Figures in parenthesis indicates change the number of camels in Rajasthan villages. (Table adopted from Jodha 1990b).

The most significant change in livestock composition is reflected by the substantial increase in the number of goats and sheep. Small ruminants could be sustained easier on degraded CPRs, and they fit better into changed migration patterns. In the context of reduced CPRs, migration of cattle has become more difficult than of small ruminants (Jodha 1985a, 1988b). Thus sheep and goats, often blamed of destroying vegetation in CPRs, seem to have become more important following the degradation of CPRs rather than vice versa. Broadly similar changes in the composition of livestock have been recorded by other micro-level studies (Brara 1987, Iyengar 1988, Ahuja and Rathore 1988, Blaikie et al. 1986).

6.5 SELECTIVE APPROACH TO CPRs

Research and observation have revealed that villagers have a differential approach to specific aspects of various common property resources in the same village. A good understanding of this phenomenon can offer useful leads for future strategies for the sustained use of CPRs. A detailed inquiry over 176 units of CPRs from different villages revealed the significant new aspects of CPR management.

The term "management" is defined to cover people's (as against government's) interventions for: (i) area protection, (ii) usage regulation, and (iii) development or upkeep of CPRs. Based on detailed case histories (covering a period of 30 to 40 years) of 176 CPR units, an inventory of nearly 1,450 events involving "people's interventions" in CPR matters was prepared (Jodha 1989a). The distribution of such events (i.e., CPR management events), according to the factors inducing them, is presented in Table 14. More details are summarized in Annexes 2 to 4. From these data, we can infer the following:

(i) The bulk of these specific management events are a by-product of other developments, such as adherence to certain rituals and religious sanctions, factional quarrels in the village or specific conditions of government grants to the village. For instance, if the area of any CPR helps the villagers to qualify for certain grant or relief, they try to keep its area intact. In this perspective,

Table 14
FACTORS INDUCING THE ADOPTION OF MANAGEMENT MEASURES FOR CPR UNITS[a]

Factors Underlying the Adoption of Measures	% Distribution, of Management, Events According to the Underlying Factors			
	Area Protection (474)[b]	Usage Regulation (423)	Development (532)	Total (1429)
A. *CPR-unit related factors*[c]:				
1. High productivity, visible contribution to private farming	12	12	13	12
2. Location, size, proximity to village	12	9	8	10
3. Usability for seeking government grant	15	5	20	14
B. *User related factors*:				
1. Private stake/control of influential/groups	5	12	10	8
2. Short lived provocation against irregularities, encroachments, etc.	8	11	--	6
C. *By-product of other activities*:				
1. Factional politics of village	24	25	8	19
2. Rituals/religions sanctions	5	9	3	4
3. Provisions under development/ relief programs	13	7	23	17
D. *Genuine/positive factors*:				
1. Concern against degradation, irregularities; enlightened leadership, NGO-activities	6	10	15	10

a. Source: Case histories of 176 CPR units. See Jodha 1989a for details. Also see Annexes 2 to 4.

b. Figure in parentheses indicate total number of measures adopted. Percentage distribution of these measures according to the underlying factors is presented in the respective columns.

c. These factors can be grouped under alternative categories such as: (A. 1-3, B-3) Economic; (B. 1-2, C-D Political; (C-3) Religious; (D-1), Environmental concerns and participatory processes.

the management of CPRs is tied to their usability for purposes other than their utility as community assets. Factionalism and rituals (unless used in some innovative ways) offer little usable leads for future CPR strategies. However, tying various government grants CPRs (to include their management and productivity), can be of help.

(ii) Higher productivity and yields of CPRs play an important role in inducing better management. This becomes important when these gains are shared more equally. The productivity -- management linkage offers a useful clue for breaking the vicious circle of "degradation -- neglect -- more degradation" that has characterized CPRs.

(iii) CPR unit's location (e.g., in the context of a watershed), size, and proximity to villages, as well as rituals and religious sanctions affecting specific CPRs, also play positive roles in their management. Since most of these factors cannot be easily manipulated, in general they may not provide an operational basis for future protective strategies. Yet they suggest the need for location specific measures to manage CPRs with greater involvement of the local people.

(iv) Genuine concern against degradation and misuse of CPRs is an important factor that may induce activities to maintain common resources. This accounts for a small proportion of management events in the villages studied, but offers a potentially viable option for rehabilitation works. With the involvement of NGOs, this could be further strengthened.

People's discriminating approach to different resources further reconfirms the role of local organization and institutional factors in the upkeep of community resources. However, it also suggests useful leads for macro policies which can stimulate at the village level better management of CPRs, together with other participatory processes. The lessons for CPR strategies may include the following:

(i) make CPR management an explicit part of the criteria for resource transfers to villages;

(ii) focus on productivity promoting measures, to break the nexus between low productivity and the neglect/degradation of CPRs;

(iii) differentiate the application of general CPR policies according to specific characteristics of resources units at the village level (e.g., different treatments for village forest plots which differ in size, physical accessibility, level of productivity, etc.);

(iv) develop policies and programs encouraging NGOs and other to evolve village specific measures for protecting common property resources legally.

7. FUTURE PROSPECTS: WITHER CPRs?

The evidence and discussion presented above do not suggest bright prospects for CPRs in the dry regions of India. The major factors constraining the present and future of CPRs, as revealed by the above discussion, are recapitulated under Table 15. This table also summarizes the factors which justify rehabilitation of CPRs and possible steps to do so.

7.1 CONSTRAINING FRAMEWORK

According to Table 15, the institutional arrangements related to CPRs are highly constraining. Undeclared regressive state policies, encouraging privatization and neglect of CPRs are the primary factor causing rapid decline of CPRs. Physical, legal and administrative interventions that deal with CPRs are insensitive to a CPR perspective. The response of rural people to the changing CPR situation is dominated by a tendency to grab CPR areas and over-exploit their production potential. Finally, there is neither a users' lobby nor a noise-making media to plead for CPRs.

Table 15
FACTORS INFLUENCING THE FUTURE PROSPECTS OF CPRs[a]

Constraining Framework for CPRs	Imperatives Supporting Rehabilitation of CPRs	Future of CPRs: Possible Options and Dilemma
• Undeclared, regressive state policy towards CPRs (privatization, lack of management) • People's response: land grabbing, over-exploitations, and indifference to CPRs	• Ecological, environmental, and long term sustainability concerns (i.e., required resource use systems in regions with submarginal lands and high climatic variability)	• Positive policies restricting further reduction in CPR area (obstacle -- New "Social Culture" -- collective indifference and land grabbing)
• Missing CPR-perspective of development interventions (fiscal, technological and institutional measures for CPRs)	• Complementarity of CPR-PPR based farming systems (i.e., due to non-covariability of input needs and product flows and narrow and unstable base of private crop farming)	• High investment needs for high productivity; (obstacles: long gestation period, invisibility of gains by narrow cost -- benefit norms)
• Negative side effects of development/transformation process (commercialization, etc.) • CPRs made open access resources, conducive to tragedy of commons	• Sustenance of rural poor (through product supply, employment and income generation, etc.) • Opportunity for evolving participatory development approaches	• Rehabilitation and sustaining of CPRs as high productivity community assets; (technology with focus on diversification and user perspective; management by user groups based on equal stake and equal share in gains)

7.2 RATIONALIZATION OF CPR DECLINE

Besides the above mentioned factors, a number of circumstances associated with the current position of CPRs are often interpreted to rationalize their decline. The key arguments in this regard are as follows:

(a) "Efficiency" Argument. In the context of their present depleted state and process of further degradation, privatization of CPRs is suggested as a possible solution for the physical rehabilitation and sustained productivity of these resources. This repeats the "tragedy of the commons" theory. Recent evidence from different parts of the world, however, suggests otherwise (Runge 1981; Bromley and Cernea 1989; Repetto and Holmes 1984; Ostrom 1988; Feeny et al. 1990). There is not sufficient evidence to fully analyze this issue in the context of India's dry regions. However, the prevailing situation is that CPRs in dry regions consist largely of submarginal and fragile land areas and efficient use should be defined in the context of their specific use capabilities.

Accordingly, their retention under natural vegetation (e.g., through CPR) is an effective approach for their efficient use. However, as Table 16 reveals, 78 to 96 percent of these submarginal lands were transferred to annual cropping, following their privatization. Their crop productivity performance (as compared to the prime lands traditionally cropped) is very low. Nearly half of the plots of ex-CPR land had grain yields which were 50 percent or less (Table 16) compared to the prime land plots cultivated by the same sets of farmers in the study villages. There are no data to reflect on the productivity of ex-CPR plots prior to their privatization.

Table 16
DISTRIBUTION OF PRIVATIZED CPR PLOTS
BY THEIR COMPARATIVE PRODUCTION PERFORMANCE[a]

State (Number of Villages and Ex-CPR Plots)	Proportion of Privatized CPR Area Transferred to Annual Cropping[b] (%)	% Distribution of (i) Ex-CPR Plots According to their Yields as Proportion of Yield of (ii) - Plots Traditionally Cropped [yield of (ii) = 100]			
		10-25%	26-50%	51-75%	76 + %
Andhra Pradesh (1, 65)	96	15	43	25	17
Gujarat (2, 90)	82	11	50	20	19
Maharashtra (2, 85)	93	17	61	7	15
Madhya Pradesh (2, 98)	78	12	39	19	30

a. Based on plot-wise details collected under ICRISAT's village studies; average of two cropping years (1983 and 1984).

b. This information relates to total CPR land privatized in the village rather than selected ex-CPR plots for which yield was recorded.

c. Comparison is based on observations generated by the following procedure. For each (i) - ex-CPR plot another (ii) - plot traditionally cropped belonging to the same farmer and put under the same crop was picked up. Grain yield of (i) as proportion of yield of (ii), constituted one observation. (Table adopted from Jodha 1990b)

Limited evidence based on detailed case studies of plots belonging to selected farmers in the study villages from Rajasthan and Gujarat is presented under Table 17. It shows that the grain yield of ex-CPR plots fell far short of yield from traditionally cultivated plots. However, fodder and fuel (biomass) production increased substantially in the ex-CPR plots when retained under natural vegetation. An increase of 3 to 4 times in collected biomass is quite impressive. Table 17 also reveals two additional factors associated with the increased bio-mass productivity of ex-CPR plots.

Table 17

IMPACT OF PRIVATIZATION ON BIO-MASS PRODUCTIVITY OF CPR PLOTS

Details	Production Performance of Plots[f]			
	CPR Plots	Ex-CPR Plots		Traditionally Cropped Plots
		Kept Under Natural Vegetation	Put Under Crops	
Plot (number)	6 (8)[a]	4 (5)	12 (16)	13 (16)
Capital investment[b] (Rs/ha)	Nil	300 (428)	1200 (1530)	300 (700)
Fodder/fuel collection (cart load/ha)[c]	2 (3)	8 (10)	--	--
Animal units grazed (number/ha, per day)[d]	46 (34)	7 (11)	--	--
Grain production[e] (kg/ha)	--	--	168 (203)	425 (519)
Beneficiaries households (number)	112 (81)	8 (10)	6 (7)	6 (7)

a. Based on case studies of selected plots in one village each in Rajasthan and Gujarat. Figures for the latter are put inside parentheses. Average for two cropping years (1983 and 1984).

b. Expenditure on permanent improvements, e.g., fencing, ridging, trenching during the last five years.

c. A cart load of biomass weighing approximately 5 quintals.

d. During four months of rainy season.

e. Pearl millet (Bajra) yield.

f. Area of plots ranged between one to six hectares. Plots under col. 2 to 4 had similar soil conditions. Plots under col. 3 to 5 belonged to the same farmers. (table adopted from Jodha 1990b).

Firstly, an improved production performance may come as a result of capital investment, protection, and controlled use. If the same magnitude of investment and low usage intensity are applied to CPRs, their performance too can be upgraded significantly. This has already been indicated by different studies (Shankarnaryana and Kalla 1985, Oza, 1989).

Secondly, quite obviously, privatization has restricted the access and use of ex-CPRs to a very small number of households and animals. This raises the basic equity issue, where higher production prospects for a few result in the loss of (low productivity) options for many. Moreover, in the context of limited availability of CPR lands, it will be impossible to help even a small fraction of rural population by distributing CPR lands to them. Simple calculations showed that even if all CPRs lands are distributed, in 87 percent of the study villages not more than 12 to 20 percent of the poor households can receive more than one hectare per family.

(b) "Poverty" Argument. Since the decline of CPRs is only a manifestation of a pauperization process occurring throughout the country, the solution to the former lies in alleviating rural poverty and land hunger. The further depletion of CPRs is not a solution to poverty, but their rehabilitation and regulated use is apt to contribute to poverty alleviation. The difference between employment and income from CPR-based activities in the villages with better CPRs and the others would support this.

(c) "Inevitability" Argument. As indicated by Figure 1, and confirmed by the experience of developed countries, as well as by agriculturally developed pockets within the dry regions of India (Iyengar, 1988), the decline of CPRs is part of a broader development process. The transformation of rural areas contributes to the erosion of CPRs. However, unless that transformation also reduces the heavy dependence of poor households on common property resources, the decline of CPRs in itself would only mean depriving the poor of the various services and products offered by CPRs.

Viewed this way, the utility and relevance of CPRs is undiminished in the dry regions of India at their present stage of development. Instead of their deliberate marginalization, an equally deliberate incorporation of CPRs into development programs and the consequent enhanced contributions of CPRs to rural transformation would further challenge the "inevitability argument".

(d) "Scarcity" Argument. Related to the "inevitability argument" is another reasoning based on land scarcity. In the context of rising pressure on land privatizing CPRs by legal or extra legal means is considered to be the only way to satisfy mounting land hunger. Population increase undoubtedly plays an important role in the decline of CPRs, but the population -- induced land scarcity does not seem to be a sufficient condition for decline of CPR area. At least the evidence from our study shows groups of villages with high population growth rates and yet limited decline in CPR area and, conversely, high rates of CPR decline associated with limited population increases.

Furthermore, the ultimate concern of public policies should be the elimination of hunger and scarcity of agricultural products rather than the mere satisfaction of hunger for land. The persistence of poverty even after acquiring CPR land as private property further reduces the validity of "CPR-privatization" as an answer to scarcity. On the contrary, the contributions of CPRs in terms of sustainable supplies of bio-mass and stability of farming systems may be permanently lost, and thus accentuate poverty and hunger once CPRs are privatized and converted into invariably low productivity crop lands. Other adverse environmental impacts caused by the disappearance of CPRs are also weighty considerations.

Most importantly, appropriating and privatizing CPRs, as well as overusing them, as elaborated earlier (see Table 12), are forms of forced adaptation to the declining CPR situation. They cannot be a substitute for forward looking measures to develop and harness CPRs as productive social assets. Thus, the "scarcity argument" seems to derive its validity from the default of the policy makers to develop a positive approach to CPRs.

7.3 POSITIVE CONSIDERATIONS

There are other positive considerations supporting the case for CPRs. They relate to the functions and services of CPRs as indicated by tables 1, 2, 3, and 4. They are: (i) the ecological and environmental imperatives of natural resource management in dry regions; (ii) CPR-PPR (private property resource) complementarities; and (iii) sustenance needs of the rural poor. There is yet another, more fundamental issue which relates to the rising concern to incorporate grass root democracy and traditional wisdom into the conventional development culture.

Ecological and Environmental Imperatives. Both heterogeneity of land resources and highly variable climatic conditions call for diversified resource use and keeping submarginal/fragile lands under low intensity uses (e.g., natural vegetation as against annual cropping). Provision of CPRs help satisfy the above requirements. The same goal can be achieved without help from CPRs if privatized CPRs are retained under natural vegetation. However, as shown by Table 16, where 78 to 96 of submarginal lands shifted to crops following their privatization, it does not seem likely that the PPR's would perform CPRs' ecological function.

Furthermore, the stability and productivity of environmental resources in the dry land context is greatly influenced by the way fragile resources (e.g., CPRs) are managed and protected

(Jodha 1991). A loss of CPRs would mean a loss of an important means to handle the environmental problems in dry areas.

CPR-PPR Complementarity. Due to the different production cycle of their natural vegetation, CPRs have input needs and output flows that are qualitatively and temporally different from those of private property-based crop farming. This forms the basis of the complementarities between production systems based on CPRs and PPRs (Table 4). To the extent that natural vegetation on CPRs facilitates the above complementarities, keeping part of the private land under natural vegetation can perform this function. But it is not the natural vegetation alone, but accessibility to it, which is responsible for CPRs ability to serve as a cushion when PPRs fail to meet needs (Table 17). In such a situation, there are no ready alternatives to CPRs to maintain and strengthen PPR-CPR complementarities and ensure the associated benefits, especially in the high risk environment of dry tropical areas.

Sustenance of Rural Poor. The most pressing requirement of the day is the contribution of CPRs towards the sustenance of the rural poor who lack reliable alternative options (Table 3). Notwithstanding a number of measures initiated to help the rural poor, there are not many poverty relief programs that can match CPRs (Jodha 1986). Enhanced productivity and regulated use can go a long way in raising CPR contributions to rural poor. The cost of abolishing CPRs, in terms of foregone opportunities for gains to the poor, would be too high to be compensated by other means.

8. PROMOTING THE CPR CAUSE: ADVOCACY AND ACTION

8.1 THE BASIS FOR HOPE

The present paper, though focussed on CPRs, has raised several basic issues opposed to the conventional development culture that characterizes public interventions. Conventional approaches tend to put greater emphasis on information as against understanding, on technology at the cost of institutional factors, and on the role of state or formal agencies as key actors at the expense of the role of user groups. There is an increasing concern about the side effects of these tendencies (Feeny et al. 1990). The need to incorporate local concerns, gender issues, participatory development, and sensitivity to people's perceptions and traditional wisdom is increasingly voiced. CPRs offer an ideal field to test these concerns and evolve options for wider use in government led development programs by involving people's participation, local management of local resources and other elements of alternative models.

In this concluding section we largely summarize the major highlights of the present discussion with a focus on their policy and program implications. We also allude to the major actors, including donor groups, that can make a significant contribution towards the rehabilitation and sustained use of CPRs.

The case for CPR development is based on the many contributions of these resources to human development, rather than on any sentimental traditionalism favoring the maintenance of collective resources. Objective realities make a strong case for the promotion of CPRs as a part of rural development strategies in regions like the dry tropical parts of India.

Firstly, visible and "invisible" gains from CPRs, as reported in this paper and other studies, far exceed the conceivable disadvantages associated with CPRs. The so called "tragedy of the commons" theory becomes a self-fulfilling prophesy when CPRs are converted into open access resources through default on the part of public policies (Bromley and Cernea 1989, Feeny et al. 1990).

Secondly, CPR-centered policies and programs would have a strong convergence with the policy focus of other strategies currently promoted by developing countries and donors alike. Examples include a whole range of anti-poverty programs in rural areas, measures directed to environmental stability, strategies for encouraging participatory development and sustainable resource use, etc.

Thirdly, most of the processes contributing to the decline of CPRs can be controlled through appropriate changes in public policies and other circumstances affecting these resources.

Finally, the world community (including the developing countries) has accumulated sizeable evidence on successful management of common resources through community involvement for equitable gains. This offers hope for redesigning management systems for CPRs.

8.2 KEY AREAS OF ATTENTION

The key areas where awareness, advocacy, and action must be focussed for CPR development are: public policies, technology, investments and effective involvement of users in CPR management.

CPRs and Public Policies. As stated earlier, one of the primary reasons for the decline of CPRs in the dry regions of India is the indifference of public policies towards these resources. To alter this situation, the policy environment needs to change. This could happen in three directions:

(i) Positive CPR-Policies. Policies and programs are needed to restrict further curtailment of CPR areas; for regulating the use-intensity of resources; for penalizing violations; and for empowering people (e.g., user groups) to manage resources.

(ii) Side Effects of Development Interventions. Various welfare and development interventions are undertaken without evaluating their potential impacts on CPRs. Programs ranging form land reforms to subsidies for agricultural mechanization fall under this category. Provision of some policy "riders" in terms of projects' CPR sensitivity can go a long way towards safeguarding the commons and their productivity.

(iii) General Development Policies. Many ongoing policies and programs relating to environmental protection or poverty alleviation contain elements which could be more effectively implemented if measures to protect common property resources would be included as a project component. The basis for such measures are potential contributions of CPRs to development.

However, while suggesting the above policy approaches, one should be aware of the circumstances which may obstruct the initiation and implementation of such policies. In the Indian context, the policy makers' high propensity for populist programs may prove a key obstacle since the distribution of CPR land to the people has always been used as a means to please the people. Similarly, minimization of the side effects of development interventions on CPRs, or the incorporation of common property components in other development projects may be obstructed by the indifference of program planners. A "social culture" that has favored collective indifference towards CPRs and individual tendencies to appropriate or over exploit them is another hurdle. One possibility to counteract such obstacles is to develop a strong CPR lobby through media and NGOs.

Investment Needs. Increasing the productivity of the commons is essential, and this requires protection, regulated use and investments. For converting CPRs from natural assets available for extraction only into managed productive assets, planned investment is unavoidable. The key obstacles to higher investments include: (i) absence of a fiscal tradition to patronize such community resources; (ii) a long gestation period and complex transaction costs associated with resource allocation to CPRs; and (iii) "invisibility" of gains. The solution to these problems may lie in a deliberate decision on resource transfers for CPRs and in the organization of effective user groups. Donor agencies can play an important investment role, but to do this effectively they have to incorporate a "CPR-perspective" in their approach to development and the environment.

Technology Focus. It hardly needs to be reiterated that the present degradation of CPRs is partly due to the operation of a vicious circle involving "degradation-neglect-further degradation". As discussed earlier, people can be induced to change their approach to CPRs once these are more productive. To break the above vicious circle, new technologies which can enhance regeneration, increase the flow of biomass, and improve the physical status of CPRs are an important requirement. Rehabilitation of CPRs as productive social assets requires a new technological focus in term of species, inputs, and technical methods of resource management. Diversity and usability of products need emphasis. The key obstacles in this respect are: (i) persistent gaps between the perspectives of the technologist and resource users; (ii) inability to screen available resource-centered technologies for their institutional acceptability; and (iii) high priority assigned to commercial considerations while designing technologies for community lands (as in the case of social forestry programs). Again, the remedial measures should start with the sensitization of scientists and planners to the essence of CPRs. Some work already initiated under the World Bank assisted watershed development projects has helped scientists to reorient their technologies to suit CPRs (World Bank 1989; Arnold and Stewart 1989, 1991).

Management and Regulation. In a way, rehabilitation of CPRs is less of an investment and technological problem and more a resource management problem. Impacts of investment and technology may prove short lived unless management and usage aspects of CPRs are effectively handled. In most areas, even natural regeneration itself can make CPRs more productive, provided it is permitted through the controlled and regulated use of resources. However, this cannot happen unless CPRs are reconverted from open access regimes to true common property regimes. In practical terms, this would mean re-establishing and enforcing usage regulations and user-obligations (Jodha 1985a, 1985b).

At an aggregate policy level, this could be facilitated by some provisions which would not only give legal sanction to adequate usage practices, but would also empower local communities to implement such provisions. Undoubtedly, some of these provisions in terms of a mandate to village *panchayats* already exist. But as mentioned earlier, *panchayats* have failed to implement such provisions. One reason for this failure is the legal and formal status of *panchayats* which makes them a small scale replica of state authority rather than a representative body of CPR users. Consequently, village *panchayats* failed to replace the traditional management system of CPRs (Brara 1987, Jodha 1985b) and common property resources became open access resources. However, a redeeming feature of the current situation (as revealed by the inter-village differences in people's approach to

CPRs) is that there still are certain elements which could be integrated into workable strategies for CPR management. The focal point of such strategies could be the organization of CPR-user groups.

8.3 CPR-USER GROUPS FOR ROLLING BACK OPEN ACCESS PRACTICES

The idea of CPR-users group in a way recommends itself. First, it fits well into increasingly emphasized grass root level democratization of resource management systems and participatory development (Cernea 1989). Second, this could be an important way to reduce the cost of policing and subsidizing resources and facilitate local resource mobilization. Third, it contains equity oriented elements.

However, the above positive factors could be easily counter balanced by just one factor, i.e., the difficulties of creating user groups. Left to the legal and administrative capabilities of the state, structures like village *panchayats* can be easily created. But they will be of limited use. The creation of genuine user groups calls for close understanding of various social and cultural features of village communities and their response strategies to the new forces of change (Cernea 1989). Size of group, its operational integrity, approach to internal equity, etc., are features which cannot be imposed through a generalized scheme of promoting CPR user groups. The groups have to develop in keeping with the local socioeconomic and resource-related circumstances. Without imposing specific models, state policies can facilitate this task by providing legal flexibility and logistic support for various NGOs which, with their better feel of the field and close association with village communities, can help organize locally suited CPR user groups.

There are no unique models to pattern such groupings in dry areas. The choice of the key characteristics of CPR-user groups can be based on some understanding of traditional forms of rural cooperation, a few insights revealed by the emerging patterns of CPR management (Table 14), and experience of a number of successful initiative tried for management of community resources in different parts of the country (Mishra and Sarin 1987, Chopra et. al. 1990, Shah 1987, Odell 1982, Agarwal and Narain 1990, Proffenberger 1990). Experience from other developing countries (Bromley and Cernea 1989) can also be of great help in this regard.

Based on the above, we indicate some features of prospective CPR user groups for dry regions of India:

(i) The first and foremost attribute of a CPR-user group should be equity of access and benefits from CPR for all members.

(ii) CPR-user groups should have legal status, but they should be outside the control of formal institutions such as village *panchayats*, government's revenue department, etc.

(iii) Depending on the type of CPR and location-specific circumstances, the membership may comprise the whole village community or special subgroups.

(iv) Preconditions for membership in the group (besides being resident of the village and user of CPR) should include binding commitment to user obligations and usage regulations.

(v) To ensure stability of user-groups, flexibility in terms of exit and entry of members may be allowed, with entitlements to exclusion of other villagers or outsiders from resource use.

(vi) The establishment of CPR user groups can be viewed as an intermediate arrangement in between complete privatization and current usage systems which are tantamount to open access regime. The arrangements, however, should relate to access and usages, without claim to the resource itself.

(vii) Except for the broad features described above, CPR user groups need not have a uniform pattern all over the dry regions or even throughout a single state. Depending on the specific resource-type and on village specific circumstances, the pattern may vary and evolve.

Given the dominant features of the current situation, the above suggestions may sound utopian. Factors which may obstruct the growth of user groups are: (i) the tendency of the state to limit and control people's initiatives and activities; (ii) the increasing internal differentiation of rural communities and its impacts on operation of village level initiatives (Cernea 1991). However, despite such potential obstructions, recent successful initiatives in the management of community resources by user groups and NGOs do inspire some hope. Besides, the emerging awareness and grassroots level pressure for local control of local resources and for associating people in protecting their immediate environment may also lend some strength to the case for CPR user groups.

8.4 ROLE OF DONOR AGENCIES

The past record shows that donor agencies have been virtually as indifferent to CPRs in India as the national agencies. Despite evidence of the former's ability to influence policies of national agencies in various sectors, they have not had a noticeably positive impact in the case of CPRs. In their substantial support to programs involving natural resources (e.g., community pastures, social forestry, etc.), the key focus had been on techniques and funding rather than on resource users. Importantly, however, such gaps are increasingly identified and recognized by donor agencies themselves as revealed by several evaluation exercises (Cernea 1991; Bromley and Cernea 1991; World Bank 1989; Arnold and Stewart 1989).

Besides the realization of the above gaps, a few other factors may facilitate an evolution of active CPR-policies on the part of major donor agencies like the World Bank. They would include emerging concerns such as: local management of local resources and participatory development; environment friendly patterns of natural resource use, involving people's participation at the grass root level; self-sustaining approaches to poverty alleviation, etc. Such donors' concerns are complemented by the similar concerns emphasized by the national agencies (though at times fluctuating with the degree of economic and political perturbations they are facing). In the Indian context, initiatives by agencies such as the National Wasteland Development Board (SPWD 1991), Planning Commission (Jodha 1989a) and several NGO groups (Shah 1987, Proffenberger 1989) have already attempted to incorporate CPR perspectives into the development interventions.

The more concrete areas where donor agencies could play important roles are (i) sensitizing national agency policies vis a vis CPRs (by adding CPR-riders to relevant programs); (ii) support for research and technology relevant to the CPR context; (iii) investment facilities focussed on CPR development; (iv) support to institutional measures such as promotion of user groups and relevant NGO activities.

There are two important constraints to the donor agencies' positive support to CPRs. Firstly, as in the case of national agencies, unless donor group representatives are sensitive to CPR perspectives, the case for CPRs will not get adequate and effective projection in their (feasibility, evaluation) mission reports. This is largely a matter of the professional composition of missions and their TOR, and could be handled more adequately once higher level policy issues are clear.

The second problem of donors' approach to CPRs relates to the possible incompatibility between the scale of large donor's initiatives and the diversified and the small scale of CPR activities. By the very nature of their operational style, the large donors may find CPR cases too small and uneconomic to handle or process. One approach to such structural problems could be the provision of sufficient flexibility in large grants at operational stage. Another approach may include some forms of sub-contracting jobs to small agencies carrying out small scale activities. The above approaches are already tried by some donor agencies and they could be considerably extended.

CONCLUSION

This paper has argued that common property resources play an important role in India in assuring the livelihood of the rural poor. The breakdown of common property management systems thus not only causes environmental harm as these resources are severely degraded under open access regimes, but social harm as well as the poor can no longer depend on them. For many villages in dry land India, this has increasingly turned out to be a common tragedy of environmental collapse and pauperization of the already poor.

If the trend of development in India has been to underestimate this vital resource at best and to accelerate its decline at worst, there are signs that changes in development thinking are starting to appear. There is a growing recognition that further conversion of common property regimes into open access regimes is profoundly detrimental to development and the environment. There is also a growing recognition that the small, flexible, and decentralized forms of resource management that characterize the well functioning CPRs provide the models of an important development tool.

The paper has also argued, however, that adapting traditional indigenous institutions to today's development demands is not a simple question of adapting existing local institutions to a different context. In many areas the social relationships and normative structures that have managed CPRs have frayed or snapped; in others, new demands place unfamiliar stresses that they cannot assimilate. If locally managed CPRs are to be part of the development process, research and action are needed to discover how adequate forms of social organization can be fortified or revived.

The paper has also argued that to succeed, a strategy of protecting and developing common property resources must extend well beyond user groups and grassroots organizations. Identifying and correcting the policies that have brought about the decline of CPRs is a high priority. These have included development interventions that hand out larger shares of these resources to the rich on the one hand, and populist political programs that are economically inefficient, on the other. Mostly, they have included policies that have eroded and transferred away the strength of social organization patterns suited to common property regimes over natural resources.

Understanding of the role of common property resources in rural society has suffered severely from theoretical bias and inadequate analysis. Whether the deterioration of common property resources can be halted and reversed or whether it will be another missed opportunity for India and other developing countries will depend on the will and commitment of governments, donors and society. The data from India's dry lands show what will be lost if common property institutions disappear. Whether they can be saved remains an open question.

Annex 1

THE LOCATION AND AGRO-CLIMATIC FEATURES OF THE AREA COVERED BY THE CPR STUDY[a]

State/District	Taluka/Tehsil	Number of Villages	Rainfall[b] mm	Soil Type[c]	Proportion of CPRs to Total Area of Villages (%)	Density of Rural Population[d]		
						Persons/Km^2 of Total Area in		Per 10 ha of CPRs Area in the Village
						Taluka	Villages	
Andhra Pradesh								
Anantpur	Anantpur	2	563	A-L, G	15	90	106	71
Mahbubnagar	Athmakur,							
	Kalvakurthi,							
	Mahbubnagar,	5	721	A-D, A-L	9	124	162	186
Medak	Medak	3	834	A-D, V-D	11	177	158	145
Gujarat								
Banaskantha	Kankreja,				10	210	201	205
Mehsana	Vadgam	5	655	S				
Sabarkantha	Sidhpur,				11	340	332	301
	Vijapur	5	633	S	12	238	253	208
	Prantij	5	739	S, V-M				
Karnataka	Bhalki,							
Bidar	Bidar,							
	Humnabad	3	907	A-M, A-D	12	162	137	113
Dharwar	Kalghatgi	3	691	A-M	10	134	156	154
Gulbarga	Gulbarga	3	702	V-M, A-D	9	106	129	146
Mysore	Gundulupet	3	680	A-M	18	106	103	55
Madhya Pradesh								
Mandsaur	Mandsaur	4	847	V-M	22	142	116	51
Raisen	Gairatgunj	6	1181	V-M	23	82	91	41
Vidisha	Vidisha	4	1134	V-M, V-L	28	91	98	38
Maharashtra								
Akola	Mangrulpir,		840	V-M	11	116	145	130
	Murtizapur	5	727	V-M, G	15	128	114	76
Aurangabad	Aurangabad	4						
Sholapur	Akkalkot,							
	Mohol,							
	Sholapur (N)	4	667	V-D, V-M	19	122	4	59

(continued)

Annex 1 (continued)
THE LOCATION AND AGRO-CLIMATIC FEATURES
OF THE AREA COVERED BY THE CPR STUDY[a]

State/District	Taluka/Tehsil	Number of Villages	Rainfall[b] mm	Soil Type[c]	Proportion of CPRs	Density of Rural Population[d]		
						Persons/Km[b] of Total Area in		Per 10 ha of CPRs Area in the Village
					Taluka to Total Area of Villages (percent)		Villages	
Rajasthan								
Jalore	Sanchor, Bhinmal	5	421	S	18	67	98	54
Jodhpur	Jodhpur	3	319	S	16	68	81	50
Nagaur	Jayal	3	389	S, G	15	71	73	48
Tamil Nadu								
Coimbatore	Coimbatore, Palladam	4	718	A-L, S	9	250	361	402
Dharmapur	Dharmapuri, Pennagaram	3	844	A-L, S	12	286	210	169

a. Based on district, Taluka and village records and field work in the villages during 1982-85.

b. Average annual rainfall of the nearest rain gauge stations of the study villages

c. Soil types: S = Sandy and/or sandy loam, G = Gravelly, A = Alfisol (red soils), V = Vertisol (black soils), D = Deep, M = Medium deep, L = Shallow

d. Population and area data relate to 1981

Source: Table adapted from Jodha (1986).

Annex 2
MANAGEMENT OF CPRs: MEASURES DIRECTED TO PROTECTION OF THE AREA CPR UNITS IN THE STUDY VILLAGES[a]

Management Measures and other Details	Number of Measures (Events) for Different CPR Types						
	Comm. Pasture	Comm. Forest	Waste Land	Watershed Drainage[b]	Threshing/ Dumping Ground	Water Ponds, Catchment	Total
Complaint/protest against:							
• Manipulation of land records	12	7	4	35	20	6	84
• Encroachment by people	17	14	15	32	24	12	114
• Encroachment by government	7	10	4	8	8	7	44
• Formula transfer of CPR area	9	5	7	11	12	9	53
Litigation against privatization of CPRs	8	6	--	10	6	6	36
Factional fights over privatization of CPR	10	7	6	7	18	8	56
De-privatization of privatized CPR	6	4	--	12	15	4	41
Panchayat resolution for CPR-area protection	2	3	--	--	4	--	9
Nomination of hon. custodian watchman	8	4	3	3	13	6	37
TOTAL	79	60	39	118	120	59	474

a. Source: Case histories of 176 CPR-units covering a period of 30 years ending 1982, conducted during the field work for Jodha (1986).

b. Includes river/rivulet banks.

Table adapted from Jodha (1989a).

Annex 3

MANAGEMENT OF CPRs: MEASURES DIRECTED TO USAGE REGULATION OF CPR UNITS IN THE STUDY VILLAGES[a]

Management Measures and other Details	Number of Measures (Events) for Different CPR-Types						
	Comm. Pasture	Comm. Forest	Waste Land	Watershed Drainage[b]	Threshing/ Dumping Ground	Water Ponds, Catchment	Total
Protest/action against:							
• Cutting trees/ bushes from CPRs	7	18	6	28	7	9	75
• Removal of top soil from CPRs	9	6	4	12	--	--	31
• Blocking access to CPRs by village influential	14	12	6	27	22	6	87
• Trespassing by outsiders, irregularity in product auction	18	21	3	20	--	--	62
Litigation/factional fight on misuse of CPRs	9	17	3	8	23	15	75
Village meeting to stream line auction procedure[c]	3	1	--	--	--	5	9
Agreement on periodical closure of CPR	12	8	9	--	--	10	39
Provision of penalty for outside trespassers	17	16	12	--	--	--	45
TOTAL	89	99	43	95	52	45	423

a. Source: Case histories of 176 CPR-units, covering a period of 30 years ending 1982, conducted during the field work for Jodha (1986).

b. Includes river/rivulet banks.

c. Auction of fuel/dung collection rights, lopping of trees, etc.

Table adapted from Jodha (1989a).

Annex 4

MANAGEMENT OF CPRs: MEASURES DIRECTED TO DEVELOPMENT OF CPR UNITS IN THE STUDY VILLAGES[a]

Management Measures and other Details	Number of Measures (Events) for Different CPR Types						
	Comm. Pasture	Comm. Forest	Waste Land	Watershed Drainage[b]	Threshing/ Dumping Ground	Water Ponds, Catchment	Total
CPR product auction, investment of revenue on CPR	19	20	4	3	12	16	74
Seeking government grant for CPRs	30	24	7	9	8	20	98
Contribution of CPR uplift							
• Cash	4	3	--	--	--	9	16
• Labor	22	12	7	17	10	14	82
• Others	6	3	--	--	7	4	20
Physical work on CPR							
• Fencing	9	12	--	6	12	--	39
• Trenching	12	7	3	9	--	--	31
Desilting/cleaning	--	--	--	11	--	12	23
Planting/protecting of trees	6	15	10	7	14	8	60
Linking contribution to CPR uplift to other rituals/practices	6	9	--	--	10	13	38
Maintaining village bull by CPR-revenue	9	8	--	13	9	12	51
TOTAL	123	113	31	75	85	108	532

a. Source: Case histories of 176 CPR units, covering a period of 30 years ending 1982, conducted during field work for Jodha (1986).

b. Includes river/rivulet banks.

Table adapted from Jodha (1989a).

REFERENCES

Agarwal, A. and Narain, S. 1990. *Towards Green Villages*. Center for Science and Environment, New Delhi.

Ahuja, K. and Rathore M.S. 1987. *Goats and Goat Keepers*, Printwell Publishers, Jaipur, Rajasthan.

Ananthram, K. and Kalla J.C. 1988. Eco-Sociology of Range Resources: Spatial and Sectoral Interference in Managing the Rangeland Resource in Arid Rajasthan. Paper Presented at the *Third International Rangeland Congress*, 7-11 November, 1988, New Delhi.

Arnold, J.E.M and W. Stewart. 1989. *Common Property Resource Management in India: A Desk Review*. Report for the Asia Environment and Social Affairs Division and the India Agriculture Division. The World Bank, Washington D.C.

Arnold, J.E.M. and Stewart, W.C. 1990. *Common Property Resource Management in India* Tropical Forestry Paper No. 24. Oxford Forestry Institute. Oxford: Oxford University.

Berkes F. (ed). 1989. *Common Property Resources: Ecology and Community based Sustainable Development*. Belhaven, London.

Blaikie, P.M., Harriss, J.C. and Pain, A.N. 1985. *The Management and Use of Common Property Resources in Tamilnadu*. Overseas Development Administration, London.

Brara, R. 1987. *Shifting Sands: A Study of Rights in Common Pastures*. Institute of Development Studies, Jaipur.

Bromley, D.W. and Cernea, M.M. 1989. *The Management of Common Property Natural Resources: Some Conceptual and Operational Fallacies*. World Bank Discussion Papers, No. 57. The World Bank Washington D.C.

Bromley, D. W. and Chapagain, D. 1984. The Village Against the Center: Resource Depletion in South Asia. *American Journal of Agricultural Economics* Vol. 66 No. (5) (December).

Cernea, M. M. 1991. *Putting People First: Sociological Variables in Rural Development*, 2nd edition, revised and expanded. Oxford University Press, London and New York (see, in particular, Chapter 1).

Cernea, M. M. 1989. *User Groups as Producers in Participatory Afforestation Strategies*. World Bank Discussion Paper No. 70. Washington D.C.: World Bank.

Dani, A.A., C.J.N. Gibbs and D.W. Bromley. 1987. *Institutional Development for Local Management of Rural Resources*. Honolulu: East-West Center.

Chambers, R., Saxena, N.C., and Shah T. 1989. *To the Hands of the Poor: Water and Trees*. Oxford and IBH Publishing Co. Pvt. Ltd., New Delhi.

Chen, M. 1988. Size, Status and Use of Common Property Resources: A Case Study of Dhevdholera Village in Ahmedabad District, Gujarat, Paper Presented at *Women and Agriculture Seminar*, Center for Development Studies, Trivendram, Kerala.

Chopra, K., Kadekodi, G.K. and Murty, M. N. 1990. *Participatory Development: People and Common Property Resources*. Sage Publications, New Delhi.

Ciriacy-Wantrup, S. V. and Bishop R. C. 1975. 'Common Property' -- A Concept in Natural Resources Policy, *Natural Resources Journal* Vol 15 (October).

Doolette, John and Magrath, William. 1989. *Watershed Development in Asia: Strategies and Technologies*. Technical Paper No. 127. World Bank, Washington, DC.

Feeny, D.F. Berkes, B.J. McCay and J.M. Acheson. 1990. The Tragedy of Commons: Twenty-two Years Later. *Human Ecology* 19 (1).

Gadgil, M. 1985. Towards and Ecological History of India. *Economic and Political Weekly* Vol. 20 (45-47) Special Number.

Gadgil, M. and P. Iyer. 1989. On the Diversification of Common Property Resource Uses by the Indian Society. In F. Berks (ed) Common Property Resources. op. cit.

GOI (Government of India). 1990. National Watershed Development Project for Rainfed Areas (NWDPRA): Guide Lines. Ministry of Agriculture, Department of Agriculture and Cooperation. Govt. of India. New Delhi.

Gupta, A.K. 1986. Socio-Ecology of Stress: "Why Do Common Property Resource Management Projects Fail?". In *Proceedings of the Conference on Common Property Resource Management*, BOSTID, National Research Council, Washington D.C.

Gupta, A.K. 1987. Why Poor People Do Not Cooperate? A Study of Traditional Forms of Cooperation with Implications for Modern Organizations. in *Politics and Practices of Social Research* (ed) Wanger, G.C., George Allen and Unwin. London.

Iyengar, S. 1988. *Common Property Land Resources in Gujarat: Some Findings About Their Size, Status and Use*. The Gujarat Institute of Area Planning. Working Paper No. 18., Gota, Amedabad, Gujarat.

Jodha, N.S. 1991. Sustainable Agriculture in Fragile Resource Zones: Technological Imperatives. *Economic and Political Weekly 26 (13)*.

Jodha, N.S. 1990a. Depletion of Common Property Resources in India: Micro-level Evidence in *Rural Development and Population: Institutions and Policy* (eds.) Mc Nicoll, G. and Cain, M. New York: Oxford University Press (also supplement to vol. 15, Population and Development Review).

Jodha, N.S. 1990b. *Rural Common Property Resources: Contributions and Crisis*. Foundation Day Lecture, Society for Promotion of Wasteland Development. New Delhi: SPWD.

Jodha, N.S. 1989a. Management of Common Property Resources in Selected Areas of India. Paper Presented at the *Seminar on Approaches to Participatory Development and Management of Common Property Resources*, March 10, Institute of Economic Growth, Delhi.

Jodha, N.S. 1989b. Drought Management: The Farmer's Strategies and Their Policy Implications. Paper Presented at the *National Workshop on Management of Drought*, Ministry of Agriculture and Cooperation and Indian Institute of Management Ahmdabad, July 4-5, New Delhi.

Jodha, N.S. (ed). 1989c. *Technology Options and Economic Policy for Dryland Agriculture*. New Delhi: Concepts publishing company.

Jodha, N.S. 1988a. Population Growth and Common Property Resources: Micro-level Evidence from India. *Proceedings of a United Nations Expert Group Meeting on Consequences of Rapid Population Growth in Less Developed Countries* August 23-26, Population Division, IESA, United Nations, 23-26 August 1988, New York.

Jodha, N.S. 1988b. Institutional Aspects of Range Resource Management in the Arid Zone of India. Paper Presented at the *Third International Rangeland Congress*, November 7-11, New Delhi.

Jodha, N.S. 1988c. Poverty Debate in India: A Minority View. *Economic and Political Weekly* Vol. 23 (45-47).

Jodha, N.S. 1987a. A Case Study of Degradation of Common Property Resources in India in *Land Degradation and Society* (eds.) Blaikie, P. and Brookfield, H. et al., Methuen, London.

Jodha, N.S. 1987b. A Note of Contribution of CPRs to PPR -- based Farming Systems in Dry Tropical Regions of India. Paper Presented at the *Ford Foundation Workshop on Common Property Resources* May 9-11, Sriska, Rajasthan. (Limited Circulation).

Jodha, N.S. 1986. Common Property Resources and Rural Poor in Dry Regions of India. *Economic and Political Weekly* Vol. 21 (27).

Jodha, N.S. 1985a. Population Growth and the Decline of Common Property Resources in Rajasthan, India. *Population and Development Review* Vol. 11 (2).

Jodha, N.S. 1985b. Market Forces and Erosion of Common Property Resources. In *Agricultural Markets in the Semi-Arid Tropics*, Proceedings of an International Workshop, October 24-28, 1983, ICRISAT Center, Patancheru (AP) India.

Jodha, N.S. 1978. Effectiveness of Farmer's Adjustment to Risk. *Economic and Political Weekly* Vol. 13. (25).

Jodha, N.S. 1974. A Case of the Process of Tractorization. *Economic and Political Weekly*, Vol. 9 (52).

Kaul, Minoti. 1987. *Common Land in Delhi: The Bisgama Cluster Report*. New Delhi. (Limited Circulation).

Ladejinsky, W. 1972. Land Ceilings and Land Reforms. *Economic and Political Weekly* Vol. 7 (5-7).

Magrath, W.B. 1986. The Challenge of the Commons: Non-Exclusive Resources and Economic Development -- Theoretical issues. *Working Paper World Resource Institute*, Washington, D.C.

Mishra, P. R. and Sarin, M. 1987. Sukhomajri - Nada: A New Model of Eco-Development. *Business India*. Bombay, November 16-29.

Odell, M.J. 1982. Local Institute and Management of Communal Resources: Lessons from Africa and Asia. *ODI Pastoral Network Paper 14 e*. Overseas Development Institute, London.

Ostrom, E. 1986. How Inexorable is the "Tragedy of Commons"? *Distinguished Faculty Research Lecture 1986*, Office of Research and Graduate Development, Indiana University, the U.S.A.

Ostrom E. 1988. Institutional Arrangements and the Commons Dilemma. In *Rethinking Institutional Analysis and Development*. (Eds) Ostrom, E., Feeny, D. and Picht, H. International Center for Economic Growth, Institute for Contemporary Studies, U.S.A.

Oza, A. 1989. Availability of CPR Lands at Micro-Level: Case Studies of Junagadh Program Area of AKRSP (India). In *Status of Common Property Land Resources in Gujarat and Problem of Their Development* Gujarat Institute of Area Planning, Ahmdabad, Gujarat.

Proffenberger M. 1990. *Joint Management of Forest Lands: Experience from South Asia*. The Ford Foundation, New Delhi.

Repetto, R. and T. Holmes. 1984. The Role of Population in Resource Depletion in Developing Countries. *Population and Development Review* Vol. 9 (4).

Runge, C.F. 1981. Common Property Externalities: Isolation, Assurance and Resource Depletion in a Traditional Grazing Context. *American Journal of Agricultural Economics*, Vol. 63 (4).

Sanford, S. 1983. Management of Pastoral Development in the Third World. New York: John Wiley.

Shah, T. 1987. *Profile of Collective Action on Common Property: Community Fodder Farm in Kheda District*. Institute of Rural Management, Anand, Gujarat.

Shankarnaryan, K.A. and Kalla, J.C. 1985. *Management Systems for Natural Vegetation*. Central Arid Zone Research Institute, Jodhpur, Rajasthan.

Singh, R.P., Jodha, N.S. and Binswanger, H.P. 1985. ICRISAT Village Studies Management System, Economics Group. Papers Sr. No 237. ICRISAT, Patancheru 502324, A.P. India.

National Policy. 1991. *National Policy on Common Property Land - Draft Paper.* Wastelands News 6(4), New Delhi, Society for Promotion of Wasteland Development.

Vyas, V.S. and Jodha, N.S. 1974. Contribution of Dairying to Rural Economy with Particular Reference to Small and Marginal Farmers. In *Dairying as an Instrument of Change.* XIX International Dairy Congress, New Delhi.

Wade, R. 1988. *Village Republics: Economic Conditions for Collective Action in South India.* Cambridge University Press, Cambridge, England.

World Bank. 1991. *The Forest Sector. A World Bank Policy Paper,* Washington, DC.

Distributors of World Bank Publications

ARGENTINA
Carlos Hirsch, SRL
Galeria Guemes
Florida 165, 4th Floor-Ofc. 453/465
1333 Buenos Aires

AUSTRALIA, PAPUA NEW GUINEA, FIJI, SOLOMON ISLANDS, VANUATU, AND WESTERN SAMOA
D.A. Books & Journals
648 Whitehorse Road
Mitcham 3132
Victoria

AUSTRIA
Gerold and Co.
Graben 31
A-1011 Wien

BANGLADESH
Micro Industries Development Assistance Society (MIDAS)
House 5, Road 16
Dhanmondi R/Area
Dhaka 1209

Branch offices:
156, Nur Ahmed Sarak
Chittagong 4000

76, K.D.A. Avenue
Kulna 9100

BELGIUM
Jean De Lannoy
Av. du Roi 202
1060 Brussels

CANADA
Le Diffuseur
C.P. 85, 1501B rue Ampère
Boucherville, Québec
J4B 5E6

CHINA
China Financial & Economic Publishing House
8, Da Fo Si Dong Jie
Beijing

COLOMBIA
Infoenlace Ltda.
Apartado Aereo 34270
Bogota D.E.

COTE D'IVOIRE
Centre d'Edition et de Diffusion Africaines (CEDA)
04 B.P. 541
Abidjan 04 Plateau

CYPRUS
Cyprus College Bookstore
6, Diogenes Street, Engomi
P.O. Box 2006
Nicosia

DENMARK
SamfundsLitteratur
Rosenoerns Allé 11
DK-1970 Frederiksberg C

DOMINICAN REPUBLIC
Editora Taller, C. por A.
Restauración e Isabel la Católica 309
Apartado de Correos 2190 Z-1
Santo Domingo

EGYPT, ARAB REPUBLIC OF
Al Ahram
Al Galaa Street
Cairo

The Middle East Observer
41, Sherif Street
Cairo

EL SALVADOR
Fusades
Alam Dr. Manuel Enrique Araujo #3530
Edificio SISA, 1er. Piso
San Salvador 011

FINLAND
Akateeminen Kirjakauppa
P.O. Box 128
SF-00101 Helsinki 10

FRANCE
World Bank Publications
66, avenue d'Iéna
75116 Paris

GERMANY
UNO-Verlag
Poppelsdorfer Allee 55
D-5300 Bonn 1

GUATEMALA
Librerias Piedra Santa
5a. Calle 7-55
Zona 1
Guatemala City

HONG KONG, MACAO
Asia 2000 Ltd.
46-48 Wyndham Street
Winning Centre
2nd Floor
Central Hong Kong

INDIA
Allied Publishers Private Ltd.
751 Mount Road
Madras - 600 002

Branch offices:
15 J.N. Heredia Marg
Ballard Estate
Bombay - 400 038

13/14 Asaf Ali Road
New Delhi - 110 002

17 Chittaranjan Avenue
Calcutta - 700 072

Jayadeva Hostel Building
5th Main Road Gandhinagar
Bangalore - 560 009

3-5-1129 Kachiguda Cross Road
Hyderabad - 500 027

Prarthana Flats, 2nd Floor
Near Thakore Baug, Navrangpura
Ahmedabad - 380 009

Patiala House
16-A Ashok Marg
Lucknow - 226 001

Central Bazaar Road
60 Bajaj Nagar
Nagpur 440010

INDONESIA
Pt. Indira Limited
Jl. Sam Ratulangi 37
P.O. Box 181
Jakarta Pusat

ISRAEL
Yozmot Literature Ltd.
P.O. Box 56055
Tel Aviv 61560
Israel

ITALY
Licosa Commissionaria Sansoni SPA
Via Duca Di Calabria, 1/1
Casella Postale 552
50125 Firenze

JAPAN
Eastern Book Service
Hongo 3-Chome, Bunkyo-ku 113
Tokyo

KENYA
Africa Book Service (E.A.) Ltd.
Quaran House, Mfangano Street
P.O. Box 45245
Nairobi

KOREA, REPUBLIC OF
Pan Korea Book Corporation
P.O. Box 101, Kwangwhamun
Seoul

MALAYSIA
University of Malaya Cooperative Bookshop, Limited
P.O. Box 1127, Jalan Pantai Baru
59700 Kuala Lumpur

MEXICO
INFOTEC
Apartado Postal 22-860
14060 Tlalpan, Mexico D.F.

NETHERLANDS
De Lindeboom/InOr-Publikaties
P.O. Box 202
7480 AE Haaksbergen

NEW ZEALAND
EBSCO NZ Ltd.
Private Mail Bag 99914
New Market
Auckland

NIGERIA
University Press Limited
Three Crowns Building Jericho
Private Mail Bag 5095
Ibadan

NORWAY
Narvesen Information Center
Book Department
P.O. Box 6125 Etterstad
N-0602 Oslo 6

PAKISTAN
Mirza Book Agency
65, Shahrah-e-Quaid-e-Azam
P.O. Box No. 729
Lahore 54000

PERU
Editorial Desarrollo SA
Apartado 3824
Lima 1

PHILIPPINES
International Book Center
Fifth Floor, Filipinas Life Building
Ayala Avenue, Makati
Metro Manila

POLAND
ORPAN
Palac Kultury i Nauki
00-901 Warzawa

PORTUGAL
Livraria Portugal
Rua Do Carmo 70-74
1200 Lisbon

SAUDI ARABIA, QATAR
Jarir Book Store
P.O. Box 3196
Riyadh 11471

SINGAPORE, TAIWAN, MYANMAR, BRUNEI
Information Publications Private, Ltd.
02-06 1st Fl., Pei-Fu Industrial Bldg.
24 New Industrial Road
Singapore 1953

SOUTH AFRICA, BOTSWANA
For single titles:
Oxford University Press Southern Africa
P.O. Box 1141
Cape Town 8000

For subscription orders:
International Subscription Service
P.O. Box 41095
Craighall
Johannesburg 2024

SPAIN
Mundi-Prensa Libros, S.A.
Castello 37
28001 Madrid

Librería Internacional AEDOS
Consell de Cent, 391
08009 Barcelona

SRI LANKA AND THE MALDIVES
Lake House Bookshop
P.O. Box 244
100, Sir Chittampalam A. Gardiner Mawatha
Colombo 2

SWEDEN
For single titles:
Fritzes Fackboksforetaget
Regeringsgatan 12, Box 16356
S-103 27 Stockholm

For subscription orders:
Wennergren-Williams AB
Box 30004
S-104 25 Stockholm

SWITZERLAND
For single titles:
Librairie Payot
1, rue de Bourg
CH 1002 Lausanne

For subscription orders:
Librairie Payot
Service des Abonnements
Case postale 3312
CH 1002 Lausanne

TANZANIA
Oxford University Press
P.O. Box 5299
Maktaba Road
Dar es Salaam

THAILAND
Central Department Store
306 Silom Road
Bangkok

TRINIDAD & TOBAGO, ANTIGUA BARBUDA, BARBADOS, DOMINICA, GRENADA, GUYANA, JAMAICA, MONTSERRAT, ST. KITTS & NEVIS, ST. LUCIA, ST. VINCENT & GRENADINES
Systematics Studies Unit
#9 Watts Street
Curepe
Trinidad, West Indies

UNITED KINGDOM
Microinfo Ltd.
P.O. Box 3
Alton, Hampshire GU34 2PG
England

VENEZUELA
Libreria del Este
Aptdo. 60.337
Caracas 1060-A